GOLD
IN ONTARIO

Claim stakes still dot Northern Ontario.

– Queen's Printer,
Ministry of Northern Development & Mines

This book is dedicated to Prospectors John Larche and Don McKinnon, who exemplify all those men and women who search through the North country in all seasons and weather in a quest for mineral wealth and who in their success bring employment and prosperity through the mining industry to Ontario.

GOLD
IN ONTARIO

MICHAEL BARNES

Stoddart

BOSTON MILLS PRESS

Canadian Cataloguing in Publication Data

Barnes, Michael, 1934-
Gold in Ontario

Includes bibliographical references.
ISBN 1-55046-146-X

1. Gold mines and mining - Ontario - History.
I. Title.

HD9536.C23063 1995   622'.3422'09713   C95-930789-3

© 1995 Michael Barnes
Design and typography by Daniel Crack
Kinetics Design & Illustration
Printed in Canada

First published in 1995 by
The Boston Mills Press
132 Main Street
Erin, Ontario
N0B 1T0
519-833-2407 fax 519-833-2195

An affiliate of
Stoddart Publishing Co. Limited
34 Lesmill Road
North York, Ontario
M3B 2T6

The publisher gratefully acknowledges the support of the Canada Council,
Ontario Arts Council and Ontario Publishing Centre in the development of
writing and publishing in Canada.

Stoddart Books are available for bulk purchase for sales promotions,
premiums, fundraising and seminars. For details, contact:

Special Sales Department
Stoddart Publishing Co. Limited
34 Lesmill Road
North York, Ontario M3B 2T6
Tel. 1-416-445-3333
Fax 1-416-445-5967

Page 3: Miners preparing a blasting sequence in the Holt–McDermott Mine.   – American Barrick

CONTENTS

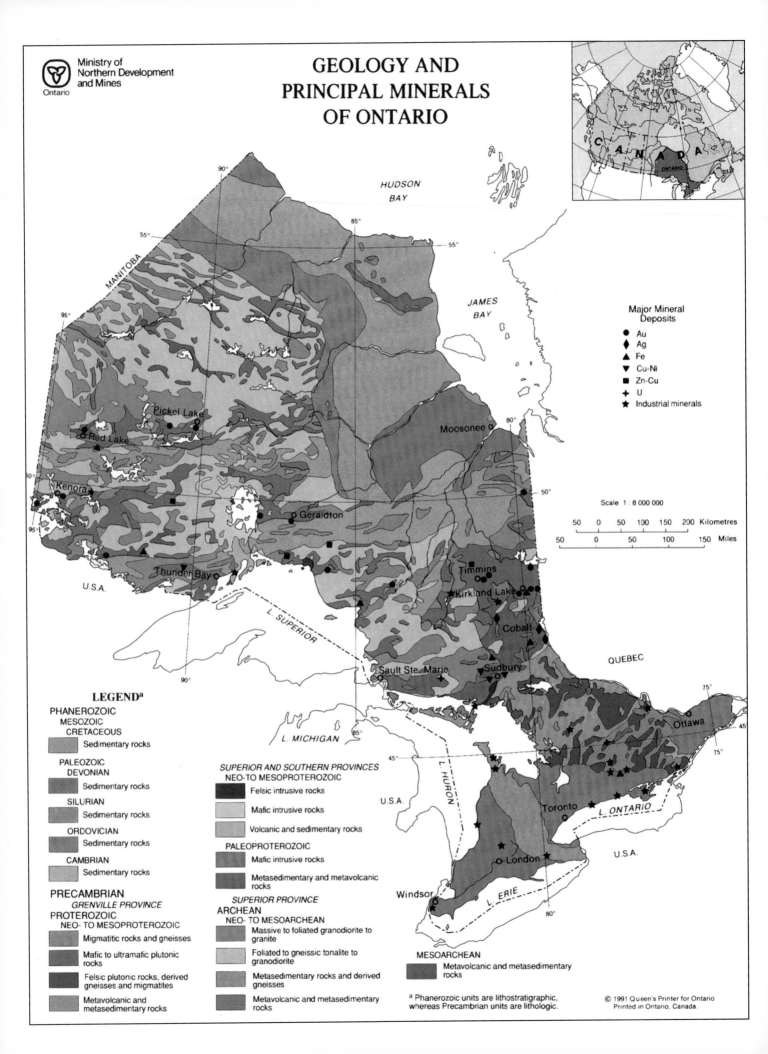

GEOLOGY AND PRINCIPAL MINERALS OF ONTARIO

Ministry of Northern Development and Mines
Ontario

HUDSON BAY

JAMES BAY

MANITOBA

Pickel Lake
Red Lake
Kenora
Geraldton
Thunder Bay
U.S.A.
L. SUPERIOR
Moosonee
Timmins
Kirkland Lake
Cobalt
Sault Ste. Marie
Sudbury
QUEBEC
Ottawa
L. MICHIGAN
L. HURON
Toronto
L. ONTARIO
London
Windsor
L. ERIE
U.S.A.

Major Mineral Deposits

- ● Au
- ◆ Ag
- ▲ Fe
- ▼ Cu-Ni
- ■ Zn-Cu
- ✚ U
- ★ Industrial minerals

Scale 1 : 8 000 000

50 0 50 100 150 200 Kilometres
50 0 50 100 150 Miles

LEGEND[a]

PHANEROZOIC

MESOZOIC
CRETACEOUS
- Sedimentary rocks

PALEOZOIC
DEVONIAN
- Sedimentary rocks

SILURIAN
- Sedimentary rocks

ORDOVICIAN
- Sedimentary rocks

CAMBRIAN
- Sedimentary rocks

PRECAMBRIAN

GRENVILLE PROVINCE
PROTEROZOIC
NEO- TO MESOPROTEROZOIC
- Migmatitic rocks and gneisses
- Mafic to ultramafic plutonic rocks
- Felsic plutonic rocks, derived gneisses and migmatites
- Metavolcanic and metasedimentary rocks

SUPERIOR AND SOUTHERN PROVINCES
NEO-TO MESOPROTEROZOIC
- Felsic intrusive rocks
- Mafic intrusive rocks
- Volcanic and sedimentary rocks

PALEOPROTEROZOIC
- Mafic intrusive rocks
- Metasedimentary and metavolcanic rocks

SUPERIOR PROVINCE
ARCHEAN
NEO- TO MESOARCHEAN
- Massive to foliated granodiorite to granite
- Foliated to gneissic tonalite to granodiorite
- Metasedimentary rocks and derived gneisses
- Metavolcanic and metasedimentary rocks

MESOARCHEAN
- Metavolcanic and metasedimentary rocks

[a] Phanerozoic units are lithostratigraphic, whereas Precambrian units are lithologic.

© 1991 Queen's Printer for Ontario
Printed in Ontario, Canada.

 Minister
of Energy, Mines and Resources   **Ministre**
de l'Énergie, des Mines et des Ressources

FOREWORD

In Ontario, the gold mining industry lays claim to a lustrous lineage that pre-dates Confederation. Indeed, the first Ontario gold mine to produce gold in quantity began operations in 1866, near Peterborough.

From its origins in southern Ontario, the gold industry has steadily expanded, primarily in Northern Ontario; such areas as the Hemlo Field near Marathon feature mines competitive with the world's best in output and efficiency.

Mining camps such as those described in this book were the source of expertise that has led to the discovery, development and production of gold in Ontario. This abundantly illustrated volume depicts the entrepreneurial drive and zeal of those who worked in the camps and who contributed to making the gold industry what it is in Ontario.

This spirit is no less alive today. Dedication and hard work will continue to provide many opportunities to improve prospects for enhanced prosperity in Ontario and boost the region's and Canada's competitive position in the mining and minerals industry.

Jake Epp

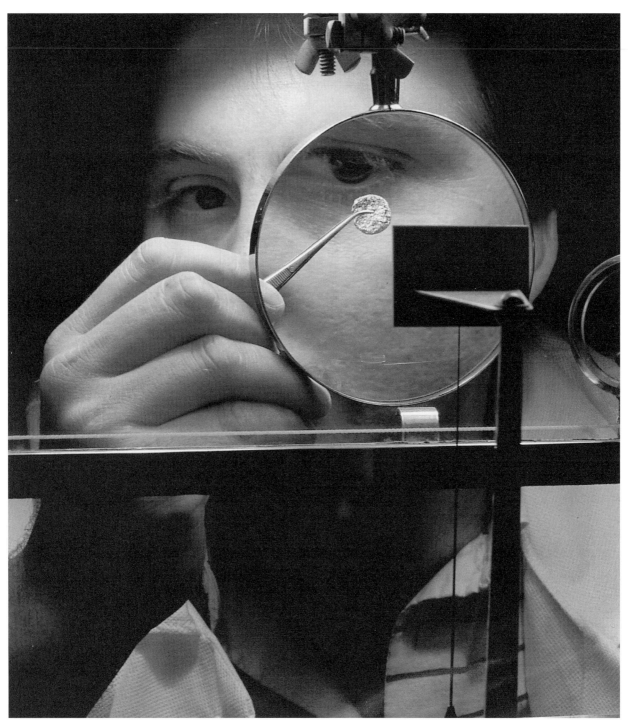

A geologist examines a gold button. – Placer Dome

INTRODUCTION

*Gold should be used to fabricate
the furnishings of public lavatories.*

VLADIMIR ILYICH LENIN

GOLD AND COPPER were the first two metals worked by man. Somewhere prehistoric discoverers saw a flake of gold in a river bed, a nugget in the ground or a seam laid bare by erosion. The sample would have shimmered and dazzled. Maybe it was kept to brighten an otherwise drab existence. Early encounters with gold must have been frequent, because it is the most widely distributed of all worked metals.

There are 460 references to gold in the Bible. The precious metal was used to decorate the Tower of Babel, and it became widespread when Croesus, King of Lydia, used it as coinage in 550 B.C. Gold has long been the ultimate possession of the wealthy and can be found in the decorations and furnishings of Tutankhamen's tomb in the Valley of the Kings. Gold has remained both popular and desirable over the centuries. In more modern times, Sir Thomas More's Utopia presented an ideal society where gold was used in everyday objects. Shakespeare made 250 references to it in his plays. People such as Benvenuto Cellini and Faberge utilized its lustrous and malleable nature to express intricate design and beauty. An Inca king found gold to be a dangerous possession. Even though he filled a room with bullion as a ransom, his captors would still not grant his life. The ultimate test to the rarity of gold came when alchemists tried to reproduce the precious metal. Many of their recipes survive — none work.

The first great American gold rush took place in California in 1849 and was made possible in part by ship and covered wagon. The Red Lake rush started with dog teams and ended with bush planes. It appeared that gold had become available to the common man. In the end, however, most of the metal wound up in corporate coffers. Goldseekers were like explorers on a new frontier. Their opportunity for exploration and adventure inspired countless people around the world who would never normally seek gold but were motivated by the thought of hitting the jackpot.

Gold and silver are the two precious metals known since earliest times. Both have been called noble for their ability to remain unchanged in various environments — resisting corrosion, oxidation and acid solutions. In ancient times it was associated with eternity because it was virtually indestructable. Gold is a bright yellow lustrous metal with a warm surface glow. It is represented by the chemical symbol Au and has a hardness rating of 2 to 3 on a scale of 1 to 10. That means harder than a fingernail but softer than a penny. Usually it is found in irregular masses, flakes or scales. Its melting point is 1,063°C. Gold is very dense and weighs nineteen times the equivalent volume of water. A cubic foot of gold weighs about half a ton.

The utility of gold is that it is the most malleable of all metals. It readily adheres to other metals and is easy to hammer and shape. The yellow metal goes a long way. One troy ounce can be drawn into wires many kilometres long. *Metric and Imperial lines inevitably cross. Imperial tons and ounces are still more commonly used in the gold industry than metric tonnes and grams, and yet metres are used for depth and distance measurement.* Jumbo jet aircraft contain gold in microcircuits half the thickness of human hair. The metal is obtained by cyanidation, amalgamation or smelting methods. It is portable and easily stored. There is just one age-old problem: gold has to be found first.

Canada is one of five countries that together produce about ninety percent of the world's gold. South Africa leads the pack, with the former U.S.S.R., Australia, the United States and Canada following behind. More than half of the Canadian output comes from the Precambrian Shield in Northern Ontario. So far, Ontario has produced about 145 million ounces of gold since mining started late in the last century. The area that continues to deliver this bonanza runs in a curving belt across the North to include such mining centres as Red Lake, Pickle Crow, Long Lac, Hemlo (north of Lake Superior), Timmins, Kirkland Lake, Larder Lake and Virginiatown.

Ontario gold was formed as a result of volcanic action, but its host rock has since been metamorphosed by heat and pressure. Some lavas of mafic or basalt composition are known as "greenstones" for their distinctive colour. Along with tuff (the compacted dust and ash of volcanic action), these coarse, highly crystalline rocks are associated with nearly all gold areas in the province. Geologists give the name Archean (or Precambrian) to the period when massive amounts of molten rock intruded into the Earth's crust, eventually hardening into quartz. Gold veins are found in this volcanic quartz. Another type of deposit is placer gold. Such a deposit is formed by water action and is present in layers of light rock or river beds. When glacial action has separated loose rocks from bedrock, the moved material is called float. Sometimes such rock contains gold. Current estimates suggest that float is usually transported no more than 1.5 kilometres from its place of origin, but a lot of gold float has been located, the source of which remains a mystery.

Twice daily during the business week the representatives of five major bullion dealers meet in a boardroom in London. Gold trading prices are compared at the N.M. Rothschild offices and, by consensus, the world price of bullion is fixed until the next meeting. Governments, investment dealers, their clients, and those in the mining industry take note of the current price. Radio and television stations in Ontario carry the London gold fix, recognizing the significance of the role played by gold mining in Canada's most populous province. Ontario produces close to half the more than $1 billion in gold mined in the country annually. Northern Ontario mines deliver almost 6 million ounces of the precious metal each year, giving employment to thousands of people and providing business to hundreds of firms in the industry and related service fields. Yet, despite its high output, Ontario's gold-mining industry is in trouble.

There is a decline in exploration and producing mines, and unemployment is rife. Investment capital is hard to find, as much of it has gone to South America, where there are fewer government controls on enterprise. Gold prices have fluctuated greatly in recent years. When the metal drops below $400 U.S., marginal mines close and development of new properties is delayed.

Mining is a risky business. Four out of five mines that started up within the past five years were losers. Seven gold mines that were successful between 1986 and 1990 cost a collective $650 million to develop. Thirty others ran a start-up tab of $1.5 billion and their cash flow was not sufficient to repay investment in the short term. The gold mine is a much bigger venture risk now than it was in the past — only one in 3,000 gets a chance at development. Generally bulk mining at a lower grade makes money today. The Williams Mine at Hemlo, for example, produces more gold in a single year than that delivered in the lifetime of some of the mining camps described in this book.

Despite the present trend toward larger mines, the tiny mines of the past have a valuable story to tell. Many of today's mines are situated on the sites of operations worked years before. In this book an honest effort has been made to mention all former gold producers. Some will be missed, as some properties were never even recorded. The Northern bush has a habit of covering up remnants of the mining past. This work covers gold mines in particular, even though gold sometimes appears as a by-product of other operations.

Gold camps are described in first half of the text, from their discovery to their present condition. Ounces recovered and grade are given where known. Grade is the average amount, in ounces, of gold obtained from one ton of ore. In some cases only a dollar amount is available. These amounts have to be considered with inflation in mind — such figures would be many times greater if expressed in today's dollars. Following the story of mines and of the harvest of gold from the rock is an account of the various players in the precious metal's path from discovery through to final production. Readers can turn to the Glossary for explanations of unfamiliar mining terms.

Gold samples are as varied as the properties from which they were taken. High-grade ore often shows no visible sign of gold because the metal is finely disseminated. Where the precious metal stands out in the host rock, it presents itself as a warm, lustrous yellow with a tint of silver. The gold industry requires optimism for the development of new mines. It must remember that for every price slump in the prized yellow metal, there is always a corresponding rise. This book shows that there is a great deal more gold waiting to be discovered in Ontario.

Today the site of Ontario's first gold mine is covered by trees and only the old incline shaft remains. – PA 50964

In 1866 Henry Vennor, geologist with the Geological Survey of Canada, identified the Richardson ore, which started the first gold rush in Ontario.
– Mines Library

A 1983 plaque unveiling. The man on the right is the grandson of the original owner of the Richardson Mine.
– Mines Library

GOLD IN CANADA WEST

*Whoever possesses gold can acquire
all he desires in this world.*

CHRISTOPHER COLUMBUS

HASTINGS COUNTY is a long, rectangular slab of land that faces Prince Edward County across the Bay of Quinte to the south and runs northwest to touch the southern tip of the District of Nipissing. The twenty-four townships of Hastings are stacked neatly in runs of three across its width. The southern third have most of the farming and development, while those to the north are sparsely settled and covered by the ancient rocks of the Canadian Shield. Soil is generally thin with much exposed bedrock and, in some cases, is covered by a veneer of glacial till. Highway 7, which runs east from Peterborough toward Ottawa, traces the boundary between the southern agricultural and the northern coarser ground.

Madoc Township is just north of this highway. Explorer Samuel de Champlain spent part of the winter of 1615 in Madoc. The township took its name from a Welsh prince who is said to have visited America in 1570. Since earliest settlement Madoc was known as a centre of mining activity. The presence of high-quality iron deposits as well as lead, marble, lithographic stone and soapstone has provided regular employment. Sixteen mines produced hematite and magnetite in the latter half of the nineteenth century. Exposed igneous and metamorphic rock in the central and northern sections has drawn prospectors, prompting mining activity. Few of the deposits have provided more than short-term return on investment, as mineral concentrations were not in sufficient quantity to prove commercially viable.

Hastings County was booming prior to Confederation. Farming and lumbering were money-makers, and small mining operations suggested a future in that industry. But the Moira River became polluted due to industrial dumping. Prosperity also brought soaring liquor sales. Bella Flint, a leading temperance champion, fought the inroads of booze for years. As far as he was concerned, a tavern was "a house licensed to make drunkards."

Marcus Powell was clerk of the local division court. Along with either William Berryman or Nicholas Snider (local accounts vary), the part-time prospector found gold on August 18, 1866. The men were trenching along a seam of copper on John Richardson's farm, 6 miles north of Madoc. Their picks broke through the limestone that held the copper and a cavity opened into a cave. In Powell's words,

"I was standing in a cave twelve feet long, six feet wide and six feet high, so that I could stand upright in it. The hanging wall was quartzite and the footwall granite, while the ceiling was composed of spar, talc and rocks of various kinds, and the floor of iron, talc, quartzite, black mica and other minerals. The gold was found in all of these rocks in the form of leaves and nuggets.... The largest nugget was about the size of a butternut." Henry G. Vennor, who later worked for the Geological Survey of Canada, happened to be in Hastings County and had occasion to identify the find. Vennor noted that Richardson's samples were of unusual richness.

Attempts to keep the discovery a secret failed and prospectors flocked to the area. Several other gold discoveries were made in the north and central townships of Hastings before the end of the year. Maps produced to service the newcomers went further than known facts and were annotated with statements such as "said to be gold here." A newspaper called *The North Hastings Mining News* advertised scores of properties for sale with the suggestion that they might contain gold. The 50-acre farm south of the discovery was subdivided into lots, and within a year there were eighty buildings in the new settlement. They called the settlement Eldorado after Sir Walter Raleigh's elusive city of gold. The place was too new for anyone to see the irony in the name — in Hastings County, gold would never be an easy mineral to mine.

Goldseekers arrived in large numbers. It is said that many paid fifty cents a night for the privilege of sleeping under a wagon in the vicinity of Eldorado. Most goldseekers came to Madoc, which swelled with service industries. The two hotels were constantly filled and unable to accommodate the influx of newcomers. Among the mining-related industries that sprang up in the city were assayers. Many were shady — not above publishing bogus results. J.T. Bell had the best reputation in this field. He was considered "the terror of the swindlers," and enjoyed a booming business.

Four coaches and two covered stages left Belleville for Madoc daily, and some visitors travelled in their own rigs. They provided custom for the twenty-six roadhouses that were hastily erected between Belleville and Eldorado. At its peak, the influx of prospectors, investors and curious spectators brought 4,000 people a month to Central Hastings. Their thirst for knowledge was filled at public addresses given by area geologists and promoters. In 1869 the County Council even established a chair of Mining at Albert College.

News of the gold discoveries spread across Canada and the United States. Many thought Eldorado would rival the success of the California gold camp. But the story of the operation of the first gold mine in Ontario by no means justified such optimism. Problems with gold extraction were overshadowed at first by the politics of development. The principal player was the Belleville Company of Citizens, led by a hotelman named Moon and two Americans — J.F. Carr and an associate named Johnson. Moon managed to spirit some high-grade from the discovery site and was able to get an investment group together easily when he displayed the ore. Carr overheard the gold talk and reached Richardson before Moon. He was in the area drilling for oil near Belleville, and his crooked nature was revealed in the way he had salted a marsh with petroleum providently brought from south of the border. Richardson gave Moon a 30-day option on 19 acres of land on his farm for

$20,000. The gullible farmer allowed Carr to take away several barrels of rich ore as samples.

Richardson never saw that $20,000 and instead began to do business with another American, named Mitchell, who had the support of local men plus two Chicago financiers, Lombard and Harding. The delighted farmer received $36,000 in cash, of which he gave Powell, the original discoverer, $16,000. Carr and the Citizens group promptly took the new owners to court in the summer of 1867. The Lombard interests won the case and formed a new company to operate the mine with an authorized capital of $300,000.

In the interval caused by litigation, a building was erected over the main shaft and an armed guard was hired to protect the place. Rumours persisted for a long time that he did a good business selling ore samples on the side. Pilfering of high-grade became so common that government geologists would later complain that they were never able to make a proper study of the ground. The Eldorado discovery sparked a lot of exploration in Hastings County. As for Richardson Mine, when it went into the development stage, investors were reported by the local newspaper to have "calmly awaited the results." These turned out to be quite different from what they had expected.

The area swelled not only with miners but also with an odd assortment of con artists, adventurers and ne'er-do-wells. A force of twenty-five mounted police was sent to Madoc to keep order. Historians have debated the origin of the force, but a photograph of the period showing their pillbox headgear suggests that it was a militia unit. When a rider came from Eldorado with the news that a near riot was taking place at the Richardson Mine, the peacekeepers under a Captain Fox were nearly put to the test. The excitement centred around one John A. "Caribou" Cameron and his mining friends from the earlier British Columbia gold rushes. Cameron had made a fortune washing placer gold in Caribou Creek and then lost it in speculation soon after. When the westerners were refused admission to the mine, they rushed it, brandishing revolvers. Some tried to tear down the gates of the property. Others even roped the shafthouse, intending to bring it down. Fortunately the mine manager allowed Cameron to inspect the works. When Fox and his men arrived, they found the mob already dispersed and Cameron enjoying a cigar in a local hotel. He explained that he was satisfied that the gold leaves and nuggets he had heard about were not a hoax. There was no more trouble and the militia returned to their barracks.

Within a year of the start of production, Richardson Mine went broke, owing $18,000. The mill was in need of repair and an attempt at reorganization failed. Shareholders were asked to surrender a portion of their stock for sale to aid the company, but few made the gesture. The mine closed was forced to close. At the close of the brief production period, the return was only $15 to the ton. Milling problems, poor operation and the pocketable nature of the ore were strong factors in the closure. Before the turn of the century, new stamp mills could break and crush the rock. Even so, Hastings gold proved difficult to treat. Heavily laced with arsenical ore, the gold was difficult to extract with an acceptable degree of purity. The county enjoyed gold fever from 1880 to 1885 and again from 1890 to 1893 with no real improvement in gold production, despite the invention of cyanide-separation.

The Sophia, or Diamond, was located near Madoc in 1913 and never made a profit.
– OA 740

Cobalt mining engineers tested the Richardson pits in 1917 without success and the property has remained dormant ever since.

Although success in Hastings gold mining was elusive, others gained from the quest for the metal. At Bridgewater, now Actinolite, a quartz mill was erected in anticipation of the custom that would flow from area mines. Its owner was Bella Flint, who also built the Temperance Hotel (he did not allow liquor on the premises). Although the mill languished for lack of feed and never did make a profit, its owner joined with others in quarrying marble. A marble church remains in the community, serving long after all the mines have been closed. Another offspring of the gold rush was the famed Peerless Drill. Patented by the Mac Machinery Company in Belleville, it served Canadian mining for many years.

There were many prospects and small gold mines in Hastings. Some, such as Ledyards near Madoc, operated briefly around 1900. Others, such as the Sophia (or the Diamond) Mine, which operated intermittently from 1896 to 1942, near Queensborough, barely covered operating expenses. A deer hunter walking out east of Flinton in 1881 found gold in quartz caught in the roots of a storm-downed tree. A group of promoters named the property Golden Fleece in a grand attempt to attract investors. Over the next 55 years the mine was operated by six firms, all without success. One operator even disappeared on his way to the site and was never seen again. During its half century of sporadic operation, the Golden Fleece had various buildings and at one time was run by an experienced company from

16

the Elk Lake mining camp. Name changes over the years, to Rich Rock Gold and Addington Mine, failed to secure investment. The mine finally closed in 1935, though there is still low-grade ore on the property.

The remains of the Star of the East or Star Mine can be found about 7 kilometres northeast of Cloyne. When it operated from 1903 to 1907, there were 5,976 tons of rock processed from two shafts. The foundations of the bunkhouse and gravity mill remain. An old safe lies embedded in one of the foundations. There may still be gold in the pyrites laced through quartz in pink dolomite. Early operators realized only $1,941 in gold over the Star's four-year life when the metal paid around $12 an ounce.

One mine that created much interest in Hastings was the Ore Chimney. Its claim was staked prior to 1909 by an Indian named Bay. The site is located on the Harlowe Road off Highway 41 north of Northbrook about 2 kilometres from the intersection. Between 1909 and 1922, two company-owned farms provided food for the cookery. About 6 kilometres away, the mine ran its own power station backed by three dams. The largest, on the Skootamatta River, was 122 metres long and 5.5 metres high. The mine, which also had a large stamp mill, was one of the biggest in the area.

The Ore Chimney had a checkered existence. In the twenties a rich pocket of gold was found but this success was offset by flooding of the power house and failure of the large dam. Although there was much development of two shafts (with an internal winze and seven levels reaching down 153 metres), the mine was a dead loss for investors. Even the name conjured up visions of money going up in smoke. One disillusioned investor remarked, "I have [even] read of the Headless Horseman, and now I have seen an oreless mine."

Much work was done in the thirties, but cash flow had a hard time keeping pace with operating plans. The place was not without expertise. The assayer had worked at the McIntyre at Schumacher, and one manager went on to run the Barry–Hollinger Mine at Boston Creek. Both the silver and gold recovered were high grade, but there never seemed to be enough to feed the mill. The property changed hands frequently until the seventies. The last news local residents received was that current owners could not agree on a financial package to reopen the mine. A good-size, solid-wood headframe remains, with mill foundations and the walls of an impressive fieldstone house. White quartz dapples the rock dump and there is evidence of recent trenching and stripping. By some, the old Ore Chimney is still considered worth a try.

The Eastern Ontario gold belt stretches 115 kilometres from Peterborough County to west of Lanark. Another group of mines within this area centred around Deloro (Spanish for "Valley of Gold"). The Tuttle, Hawkeye Red, Five Acres, the Gilmour, the Williams and, the most well-known property, the Gatling, were mines found here. Named after the brother of the inventor of the famous machine gun, the Gatling operated from 1899 to 1903. Surface deposits were rich but declined rapidly at depth. Flooding on the Moira River and problems with massive amounts of arsenopyrite, or mispickel, as it was called then, contributed to the mine closure.

Deloro went on to become a mining centre for more than 50 years, but gold became only a trace product. The Deloro Mining and Reduction Company purchased some of the old properties. It refined silver from the Cobalt camp with arsenic as a major by-product. Later the firm manufactured cobalt and steelite, which alloys cobalt with chromium and tungsten. Both products were in demand until the early sixties when competition from the Congo and a decline in silver mining closed the business. Today the Deloro plant is fenced to protect the public from tons of arsenite waste buried there. Few signs remain of the tiny gold mines that gave the valley its name.

The Belmont (later Cordova Mine) is on County Road 3, sixteen kilometres northwest of Marmora. The gold mine operated for a total of 15 years over five different periods from 1892 to 1940. H.T. Berry worked there during the last six months the mine was working. Cominco owned it then, and the mill handled 150 tons a day. Berry worked in the mill and helped with monthly smelting and pouring of gold bars. He recovered residual gold after the mine shut down and quite a bonanza was found in the agitator tanks. In half a century of production $474,548 in gold was delivered.

When mining people discuss the gold mines of Ontario, they tend to forget the discoveries in Hastings County. Yet gold has been found in twenty-seven locations spread over nine townships. Several of these have never been more than perfunctorily explored. One prospect, Sheppard's, was located on Lot 12 in Tudor Township. A preliminary assay graded at 5 ounces of gold to the ton, but the showing has been lost for some time. Recently a large deposit of gold was outlined not far from Marmora, but it is not a commercial grade. There could be a working gold mine in Hastings County soon. Canadian Mono Mines have outlined 250,000 tons at a 0.27 grade in the old Bannockburn workings north of Madoc. If production gets under way, it will be the first Southern Ontario gold mine in half a century to make money.

As for Eldorado, where the gold rush started, the only gold found now is in the cheese factory on the edge of the village. The Richardson Mine site is located on private property a few minutes' walk behind the historic plaque erected by the Province of Ontario. The low hill is heavily treed and only the pits and the mouth of an incline shaft can be seen. The ore dump is covered with undergrowth, and the place gives no hint of the excitement generated there one year before Confederation. There have been many estimates at the value of gold recovered from the mine, but they vary widely. Only the name Eldorado remains to remind us of gold fever, overpromotion and forgotten dreams.

LAKE OF THE WOODS EAST

These companies are all the same.
What have they got? An idea and a piece of rock.

BOB CROMPTON

THE FIRST GOLD FIND in Northwestern Ontario was made in the the winter of 1870 to 1871 by two Natives working for the Hudson's Bay Company. They saw a vein at Jackfish Lake, 72 kilometres southwest of present-day Atikokan. The vein was located in the Shebandowan zone, an area of Huronian schists and intrusive granites that runs west from Jackfish Lake, south of Burchell and on to the American border at Hunter's Island. Brothers Donald and Peter McKellar staked the site called the Jackfish Gold Lode. But while staking was easily done, patenting the claims was more difficult. The Manitoba boundary was in dispute between Ontario and the Dominion of Canada, and there was also a party of claim jumpers in the area. Eventually the ground was patented, but in 1881 the Manitoba boundary was extended east as far as Atikokan. The line remained there until 1889, when the western boundary of Ontario was relocated to its present position.

By 1872 the McKellar group was ready to develop its mine, but Ojibwa Chief Bluestone and his band effectively halted construction until a treaty could be negotiated with Canada. The North West Angle Treaty was the result. The property was renamed the Huronian Gold Mine but languished until the completion of the Canadian Pacific Railway in 1882 brought transportation close to the mine site. A stamp mill was built but the mine closed two years later due to high operating costs. The milling process had been unsuitable due to tellurides in the ore. The place sat idle until 1927, when it was reorganized as the Moss Lake Mine and then the Ardeen Gold Mine, before finally closing in 1936 without any profit for its owners. Only 27,168 ounces of an unspecified grade were ever extracted from the first gold mine in the northwest.

The Seine River zone extends west from Lac des Milles Lacs to Rainy Lake. Small settlements such as Bell City, Foley, Old Mine Centre, Seine River Village and Mine Centre Station grew up within this area to serve local resource development. One prime gold area was the Upper Seine River. The Harold Lake Mine, 10 kilometres northwest of Atikokan in Baker Township, operated with a five-stamp mill from 1894 to 1896. Its small and irregular veins produced $11,236 worth of gold from 1,131 tons. The plant was later destroyed by a forest fire. The drilling firm Longyear reexamined the site in 1937, but though there was more gold, it was not

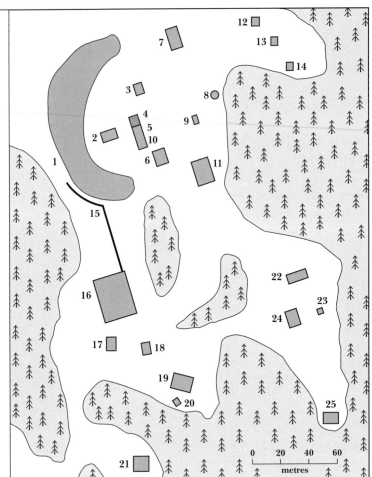

THE BIG MASTER GOLD MINE 1902

Situated in the Upper Manitou Lakes area, the layout was typical of an isolated gold mine with the bush all around the operation.

1 WASTE ROCK
2 ORE HOUSE
3 BLACKSMITH'S HOUSE
4 SHAFT
5 HEADFRAME
6 DRY HOUSE
7 POWERHOUSE (DIESELS & GENERATORS)
8 WATER STORAGE TANK
9 ELECTRICIAN'S SHOP
10 HOIST ROOM
11 COMPRESSOR HOUSE
12 OIL HOUSE
13 MAGAZINE (STONE)
14 MAGAZINE (TIMBER)
15 CONVEYOR BELT
16 MILL
17 ASSAY OFFICE
18 REFINERY
19 POWERHOUSE (BOILERS)
20 SUPPLY SHOP
21 MACHINE SHOP
22 BOARDING HOUSE
23 MEAT STORAGE SHED
24 COOKERY
25 MANAGER'S HOUSE

The Foley Mine at Schoal Lake (shown in operation in 1898) milled 7,760 ounces of gold. – PA 14073

considered viable. At the turn of the century, Anglo Canadian Estates found gold in quartz 4 kilometres northwest of the lake. About 20,000 tons of potential ore were blocked out, but by 1912 only $400 in gold had been recovered. The operation was revived in 1936 as the Elizabeth Gold Mine but had similar poor results.

The most successful of the Upper Seine River mines were the Hammond Reef and Sawbill. Both are on Sawbill Lake, about 30 kilometres northwest of Atikokan. James Hammond's claim was staked in 1894. Three years later it had a mine with a 40-stamp mill and was the largest plant in the area. Production started in 1922, and 222 ounces of gold were milled. That was the final total when the mill motor burned out in a thunderstorm and the mine had to close. The adjacent Sawbill Mine was a better producer. From 1897 to 1899, workings that reached the 83-metre level produced 677 ounces of gold. In 1938 the place was reorganized as the Upper Seine Gold Mine but did not last long.

The Hammond Reef and Sawbill mines provided welcome employment for the area. A stage covered the 56 kilometres from the CPR line at Bonheur in 11 hours. The open democrat jolted its way along a rutted track and across corduroy swamp roads. Horses were changed at Red Paint Lake due to the grueling pull. The final part of the trip across Sawbill Lake was made by scow. Enterprising Natives sold their locally made canoes to travellers in search of independent transport. Both mines had hotels that catered to thirsty travellers. James Hammond was later killed when a heavy piece of machinery he was freighting rolled, crushing him to death.

One area mine, the Sunbeam, operated between 1897 and 1905. An inscription written in French on one of its remaining doors translates, "I am here because I am lost; my destiny is that I am doomed to die here." Since there is no record of a death on the property, the words were likely penned by either a miner or a prankster. There were other mines, but other than their names — Minto, Big Six, Lily, Fissure, Mayflower, Jack Lake, Clear Lake, and Golden Winner — they have no recorded past.

The Lower Seine River is bounded by the Quetico fault to the north and the Seine River–Rainy Lake fault to the south. It centres around Bad Vermilion, Schoal and Little Turtle lakes. In its heyday, the area was accessed by steamer east from Fort Frances across Rainy Lake, down the Seine River to Schoal Lake. Today Highway 11 passes just to the south of the old camp. The discovery of gold near Rat Portage and the completion of the railway brought prospectors from the South to the Lower Seine River. In 1891 Alexander Niven, a provincial land surveyor, cut a baseline along 48 degrees latitude from the boundary of the Rainy River district to Fort Frances. This provided important reference points for mining districts.

The first discovery in the area was made by George Davis in 1893 on the American side of the border at Little American Island on Black Bay. The next was made by J.S. Campbell on the Canadian side, east of Island Bay in Vermilion Lake. This would become the Golden Crescent Mine, eventually yielding all of 75 ounces of gold in a mine that boasted two adits and four shafts. Within seven years 47 occurrences had been located, but among the resulting mines only three produced any significant amount of bullion. In September 1893 Thomas Weigand and Alexander Lockhart found a gold vein along the shore of Schoal Lake. The resulting Foley Mine had a 121-metre shaft and a 20-stamp mill and was in operation from 1897 to 1898. The second-largest producer, it milled 7,760 ounces. Americans

Ed Randolph and Neil Burger staked the Gold Star Mine, which, at an output of 11,745 ounces, became the most profitable of all the Lower Seine River mines. The property had a 162-metre shaft and carried ore by an aerial tramway almost a kilometre to its ten-stamp mill on Bad Vermilion Lake. When ore gave out, the property was salted to attract further investment. Despite this early lapse, the mine has attracted the attention of prospectors ever since. After all, it yielded a total of 9,759 ounces and mining people believe there is more in the vicinity.

The third most important discovery, on the southwest end of Little Turtle Lake, was acquired by W.A. Preston (later a member of Parliament). The mine began as the Preston and was later renamed the Olive after his daughter. It was plagued by financial difficulties and ran intermittently from 1897 to 1909, with 3,240 ounces recovered. There were two shafts, and a 292-metre tramway took ore to a 25-stamp mill. One story reports that a Native guide, Billy McGee, took a mine official who was packing some heavy boxes to Rat Portage. This led to speculation that some high-grading was being done at a senior level. Twelve other mines — Pacito, Isabelle, Ferguson, Golden Crescent, R.C. Cone, Alice A., Sundry, Stella, South Vermilion, Dinosaur–Smylie, Lucky Coon and Manhattan–Decca — produced less than 1,000 ounces between them. Ventures such as the Money Maker, Sugar Loaf, Hibernian and Lee Rosa de Ora mines were frauds, set up to fleece investors.

Rat Portage was named for the abundance of muskrats in that water-veined district. Some residents felt it was derogatory. They noted that the Maple Leaf Flour Company was discouraged from building in the town, as the word "rat" on their flour bags would not evoke a very positive image. In 1905, though a newspaper poll found "Sultana" to be the most popular replacement choice, the first two letters of Keewatin, Norma and Rat Portage were cobbled together to provide "Kenora."

The centre of the northwestern gold rush was Schoal Lake. The steamer *Wanda* made connections between Fort Frances and the small communities that grew up along the lakeshores. Rough wagon roads connected most of the mines. Mine Centre was the largest settlement. It boasted three hotels: the Rutledge (or Caldwell), the Randolph and Mine Centre. There was also a customs house, an assay office, a post office, a school, a drugstore and even a tailor shop. Although it had a population of only 500, the place was a mecca for outlying mines, which made all of these services necessary. Mine Centre added seven new businesses, including a sawmill. The village was complemented by Bell City, 2 kilometres to the west. Bell City was small, with just six streets and a hotel. The Foley Mine, 5 kilometres west of Mine Centre, was the only property with its own townsite, which included a hotel, three boarding houses, a school and about a dozen cabins. Seine City, Turtle City and Chief City were merely steamer stops. In June 1899, Mine Centre and Bell City were honoured with a visit by thirty members of the legislature and seventeen reporters. This was part of a fact-finding tour of New Ontario. Promises were made for funds to repair local streets.

Mine Centre had its share of characters. One was Jack, a barroom brawler who specialized in beating up unwary newcomers. Locals finished his exploits when a boxer from south of the border was brought to town to give Jack an easy mark. The local bully was soon whipped. Other residents who gave colour to this gold camp included Chief Neverwash, Rattlesnake Bill and a prospector called Pegleg. Pegleg must have had a spare, because his wooden limb was often displayed above the bar.

Small gold camps in the Northwest depended on waterways for transportation. Here the steamer Maple Leaf *ties up at the Tycoon Mine on June 19, 1899.* – OA 10399 16

The Lower Seine camp was only 15 kilometres from the American border, and smugglers flourished as they ferried high-grade south to avoid taxes. From 1903 to 1904 the gold rush collapsed and the mines closed down. Deposits were small and visible gold soon played out. The Canadian Northern Railway arrived to the North and named its station Mine Centre. Many residents of the original settlement moved to the new location, and the little gold mine sites disappeared except for a few buildings. The Mine Centre Hotel had a reprieve. It was dismantled and barged to Fort Frances, reappearing on the corner of Scott and Central Avenue, first as the Monarch and then the Irwin Hotel. The remains of the Lower Seine mines are now only accessible to hikers. For many years, the once-bustling area had Russell Cone as its lone resident, working his two-stamp mill to recover gold overlooked in the previous gold rush.

As Lower Seine mining activity was beginning to fail, the Upper Manitou Lakes area was just coming into its own. This gold field is located between Dryden and Fort Frances on Highway 502, about 100 kilometres north of the Highway 11 turnoff. An 8-kilometre bush road from Lake Minnehaha leads to the Gold Rock area. At the turn of the century, access was by road from the CPR station at Wabigoon. Fourteen mines were served by Gold Rock, a small settlement that grew up after 1897 on Trafalgar Bay, a marshy inlet of Upper Manitou Lake. The most significant mines were Big Master, Laurentian, Detola and Elora (or Jubilee). Big Master was the pioneer plant, and it started up on July 1, 1902. Miners were kept happy with "high western salaries" (according to the mining inspector) and they enjoyed short, eight-hour shifts. The mine produced only $5,000 in gold by the

The Mikado Mine and its mill overlooked a scenic spot on Lake of the Woods. – OA 10399 33

fall and over the next two years was plagued by lack of fuel, capital and a rapidly depleted orebody. High-grading was said to be common. By 1904, shareholders were not prepared to bankroll the company any further and the mine closed. Fortunately for Gold Rock, Anthony Blunt located a pocket of rich ore just east of the settlement. He called it the Laurentian, and this mine soon became the leading gold producer. Mining commenced in 1905 and the first gold bar was poured a year later.

The camp was dogged by bad luck. Little Master Mine kept opening and closing on almost an annual basis between 1903 and 1906. The mine was finished when its powerhouse burned. Paymaster Mine belied its name — in 1909 the owners closed the property rather than perform the safety improvements ordered by the mining inspector. Detola Mine was mismanaged by Dryden Smith, who also operated the Laurentian. Though otherwise well planned, the mine did not produce enough mill feed to keep the mill working beyond 1911. The camp was on the slide when its mainstay, the Laurentian, ran out of gold in 1909. Since there were no more mines working, Gold Rock was soon finished.

Investors were hard to snare during that period. They were wary of capital losses in mines such as Big Master. The lure of base metals and the new Cobalt silver camp drained away money from small gold concerns. The Manitou district mining revived in the thirties as labour costs fell. The four principal mines were reopened and the Laurentian mill was used to sample ore. Only Big Master gave up any gold. Its surface plant was refurbished and there was a modest bullion output, but by 1948 the mine was worked out. The bush closed in on Gold Rock and the small mines were forgotten. Some buildings were torn down, others fell and decayed, but remnants of mines and machinery still survive. Despite attempts by archeologists and architects, the province has done nothing to preserve the area. At the very least it could be used as a tourist attraction to offer a glimpse of turn-of-the-century gold mining.

There was another mining camp even closer to the Manitoba border, in the area around Kenora. The majority of activity centred in the Wabigoon volcanic sedimentary belt, which runs east and west. Other Lake of the Woods prospects were to the north, in what geologists today call the English River subprovince. In Lake of the Woods, gold was first found on Hay Island. Showings were later found on Boulder Island in Camp Bay. In 1881 the Winnipeg Consolidated Company opened a mine at Big Stone Bay, 19 kilometres southwest of Kenora. The venture's five-stamp mill closed in 1886 when unpaid miners forced a shutdown.

Most mines in this area were shallow and primitive. The CPR was quarrying stone for bridge piers and prospectors fanned out in the vicinity and found gold. In 1891 the Sultana Mine started shipping concentrate, which was tested at the Canadian Milling and Reduction Company plant at Kenora. The 40-stamp mill had a good run and delivered close to a million dollars in gold before the precious metal ran out in 1906. A host of prospectors had arrived in the area in the early 1890s. One was John Lapine, who was renowned for his long, white hair and his tales of travels in the bush. Entertainment was always welcome in the mining camps. One young minister, fresh out of England, was subjected to the inventive profanity of a teamster with a broken rig. "My dear fellow," quizzed the newcomer, "where did you learn this vile language?" With evident satisfaction, the teamster replied, "Sir, you cannot learn this language anywhere — it's a gift."

The Burley Mine set up a drill rig adjacent to the Sultana Mine. Drilling was done through the lake ice. This attracted investors because the idea was so novel to the district. A little salting helped, but shares were dumped when no commercial-grade ore was found. By 1894 the Lake of the Woods area was known for the production of caviar, but its precious metals output was not yet significant. Many small mines were optimistically seeking gold at this time, including Queen of Sheba, Minerva, Yum-Yum, Woodchuck, King and Rajah. Names such as Black Jack and Dead Broke revealed more about their owners than their property viability. A lack of spectacular earnings did not prevent the proprietor of the Russell House in Kenora from listing thirty mines within 35 kilometres of his establishment. One was the Regina (in honour of Queen Victoria), notable more for its manager, a retired Colonial general, than for its gold output. Sir Henry Clement Wilkinson lived on-site in palatial style and treated his miners as if they were in the army, parading them before and after every shift and insisting on a proper religious tone around the place. Other mines that produced no ore were the Sirdar, the Tycoon, the Bullion and the Cornucopia. One closed mine, the Argyle, had its mill dismantled in winter and shipped to British Columbia, much to the surprise of shareholders when they looked for resumption of work in the spring. Most Lake of the Woods mines were closed in 1906. News of placer gold in the Yukon and the growth of the Cobalt and Porcupine camps tempted away miners who were disgruntled by the uncertain prospects in the tiny northwestern mines.

Julian Clifford Cross became well known in later years for his role in the development of the Steep Rock iron mine, but in 1913 he was just starting out as a prospector. Before graduating from Queen's University he had worked in the bush. He thought some of his specimens might contain gold. Fellow students at Queen's switched his rocks. His hopes were dashed when a professor advised that his rocks be assayed. Cross was understandably cautious when he found rich gold float in Schoal Lake on Cameron Island near the Manitoba border. Such discoveries always led to hard work, as the prospector had to trace the float back to its source. Cross figured that, because it was on an island, the float he found might have been pushed up by lake ice and other action over the centuries and that the source might be directly below it. His perseverance paid off. Assay samples ran 5 ounces to the ton, which was unheard of in this area. The resulting Cameron Island property made a promising start to Cross's career. Other mines in the vicinity were the Mikado and Cedar Island.

The Lake of the Woods area saw an increase in exploration activity from 1932 to 1938. The Wendigo, Witch Bay, Stella-Lac, La Belle, Golden Gate, Gold Creek and Horseshoe mines ran south down the lakeshore from Kenora. Improved mining methods and a rise in bullion prices gave properties that had been worked at the turn of the century a new lease on life. The Horseshoe had a checkered career in common with most of its neighbours. Formerly the Regina, it was located on an inlet off Whitefish Bay east of the Alneau Peninsula. Since 1894, when the vein was first discovered, it had opened and closed six times. There was a shaft to the 164-metre level and a winze dropped down a further 39 metres. Few records have survived. Accounts of the mine's total output vary from $200,000 to $500,000. During the late thirties and forties, total gold production from the Lake of the Woods area was over $3.5 million, of which the major share came from the Windigo Mine on Witch Bay south of Kenora. Windigo contributed 61,164 ounces.

Approximately 180,000 ounces of gold was won from twenty-seven mines in the Kenora district from 1880 to 1976. Since there are over 331 known gold occurrences, potential for future development seems very good. Several of the former producers are now receiving renewed attention. The most successful mines, all of which operated for seven years or more, were Bully Boy, Cameron Island, Champion, Combined, Cornucopia, Gold Hill, Golden Horn, Kenricia, Mikado, Oliver, Olympia, Ophyr, Regina, Scramble, Severn, Stella, Sultana, Treasure and Wendigo. The Ministry of Northern Development and Mines has carried out extensive geological mapping to assist firms in exploring this mining camp. Bond Gold at Schoal Lake and the Scramble project in Jaffray–Melick are now being explored. The Nainsco property at Cameron Lake and the Consolidated Professor at Schoal Lake hold promise (the latter is said to have a potential annual capacity of 50,000 ounces). Big money has been spent on these two prospects and mine development is almost assured. Schoal Lake provides the drinking water for Winnipeg, hence there is a need for extreme caution in evaluating the environmental impact a mine would have on the lake. One possible solution would be to barge the ore across the lake and mill it on the mainland.

Over Atikokan way, the old Fern Elizabeth Mine is under investigation. The Atko (formerly the Sapawe Gold Mine) was a good producer in the sixties and still sparks interest. But probably the most promising area is around Moss Lake in the Shebandowan area. There is a huge deposit of low-grade gold near the old Huronian Mine, where activity in the area first began. Many more former producers, such as the Sakoose at Kawashegamuk Lake, and the Baden Powell, Bonanza and Redeemer mines around Eagle Lake, are said to be worth a second look. The Kenora district will no doubt host a major mine as financing improves. There are also many opportunities in small-scale custom and portable milling, and even heap leaching, at former mines that caused so much excitement at the turn of the century.

ALGOMA OCCURRENCES

Get you to the wild again with Wawa.

BLISS CARMAN

SOUTHERN ALGOMA has never been considered gold country. There have only been two mines east of Sault Ste. Marie. One was the Rocky Lake Mine. Apart from the name and a few faded photographs, no details of the place remain. We know more of the discovery made by William Moore in the same area that went on to become the Ophir Gold Mine. In 1894 there were thirty employees, two small shafts and a 20-stamp mill. That same year a rock burst killed three miners and an angry mine inspector found several safety infractions at the plant. The incident kept the mine closed until 1909, when it reopened as the Havilah Mine. Only 1,001 ounces were taken in the mine's lifetime.

North of the Soo, prospects were more promising. Two areas have maintained interest from the turn of the century to the present. One is in the vicinity of Wawa near Michipicoten. The other is to the northeast between Goudreau and Missinabie. Gold is usually found in the greenstones and intrusives. Renabie is the only large mine to have produced to date, and until recently Algoma has not been favoured by prospectors or promoters.

The Michipicoten–Wawa district is well known in the history of the North. An important Hudson's Bay Company post was located at the mouth of the Michipicoten River. In 1846 Dr. John Rae used this Lake Superior port for the start of his canoe trip north in search of Sir John Franklin, a missing explorer. The land adjacent to the Great Lake was long known for copper and iron deposits. In 1897 William Teddy, a Native Canadian, found gold on Wawa Lake. His wife drew his attention to the glistening metal in quartz along the shore. Teddy sold the location of his discovery to Jack MacKay of Sudbury for $1,200. In good amateur tradition, Teddy blew the lot and had to depend on charity to get back to Wawa after a brief stay in Quebec. A minor gold rush took place. Prospectors visited MacKay Point and took samples, but a mine was never built. The village of Wawa grew as a base for prospectors, who staked 1,700 claims in 1898.

The Michipicoten and Magpie rivers and a belt northward from High Falls on the Michipicoten River to MacKay Point on Wawa Lake were promising areas for gold hunters. Soo-based industrialist Frances Clergue started the Grace Mine in 1900. It was shut down three years later. Eight other small producers were worked, but poor returns saw the closure of almost all properties by 1906. Wawa became

William Teddy, the man who started the Wawa gold rush, spent his earnings quickly. – OA 746

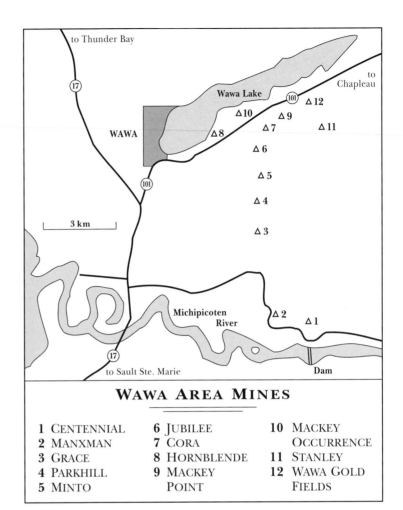

WAWA AREA MINES

1 CENTENNIAL	**6** JUBILEE	**10** MACKEY
2 MANXMAN	**7** CORA	OCCURRENCE
3 GRACE	**8** HORNBLENDE	**11** STANLEY
4 PARKHILL	**9** MACKEY	**12** WAWA GOLD
5 MINTO	POINT	FIELDS

The Minto Mine, shown here in 1928, ran from 1929 to 1942 and was a good producer. – PA 14081

The miner's families had an isolated and lonely life at the Shenango Mine, 1936. – PA 14861

the focus of iron mining in the district. The completion of the Algoma Central Railway in 1914 meant that entry to the area became easier for prospectors, and when iron declined in the early twenties, gold picked up again. Twenty-two small prospects were worked over the next 20 years.

William Teddy died in 1931 before the peak gold-mining period in Wawa. Many of the small properties in this area contained high-grade ore. Twelve have an output on record, and six of these delivered gold into the thirties. The Golden Reed, Norwalk and Hornblende mines operated from 1904 to 1910. McMurray Township has always been a prime mineral location. Here the Deep Lake Mine rendered a total of 1,663 ounces at a handsome 0.50 grade; the Smith, 536 ounces at the same grade. The Stanley, in its 1936 operation, disappointed shareholders with only 84 ounces delivered at a 0.27 grade. Ranson, Murphy and Centennial (once Kitchigami) were tiny properties with little gold, but the last produced a fine 0.70 grade.

What remains of the top producers at the Wawa gold camp may be found in McMurray Township, on a road off Highway 101 just east of town. A little community existed in the thirties at Parkhill to serve the neighbouring mines. There was even a hotel, the Parminace, named after three mines — Parkhill, Minto and Grace. The Grace (later the Darwin) operated in no less than thirteen separate time periods between 1902 and 1944. That was a long time to recover a total of only 15,191 ounces. The Minto, which took in two smaller properties, Jubilee and Cooper, worked right through from 1929 to 1942. Its 50-ton mill refined 37,678 ounces of 0.20-grade gold, which was respectable even though it was sporadically placed. The Parkhill was the top producer in the area. It opened and closed seven times between 1902 and 1944, with its most productive period from 1930 to 1938. Its 100-ton mill extracted 54,301 ounces of a good, 0.40 grade. On the same road that serviced these well-known properties, the Surluga Gold Mine operated from 1968 to 1969 and again from 1988 to 1989. The total output was 8,898 ounces.

The Renabie Mine (shown in 1950) was the only big gold producer in the Wawa area, operating until 1991, when the orebody pinched out. – MNR

Although gold was first recorded on Emily Bay on Dog Lake in 1896, the area between Goudreau on the Algoma Central Railway and Missinabie on the CPR did not become a precious metals producer until 40 years later. The Algold, Goudreau, Algoma Summit and Edwards mines were tiny outfits with relatively low grades. The Cline Mine produced 63,328 ounces of 0.19-grade gold from 1938 to 1948. None of these would come close to the volume of the Renabie Gold Mine, which was the biggest producer yet to operate in the Algoma District.

Although it had a slow start, the Renabie Mine produced for more than half a century. A local hunter, "Pegleg" Desbien, saw gold in quartz on the site in 1920 but failed to report the fact until the outbreak of the Second World War. The Saw-dust Syndicate, so named because the principals were lumber company executives, was the first developer of the property. Prospectors worked the ground, located the original showing, and diamond drilling soon commenced. Macassa Gold Mines had controlling interest by 1941. The deposit attracted attention from geologists, as it was the first property in Ontario to produce precious metal from gold-bearing granite. Wartime restrictions closed the mine from 1942 to 1946, but when it reopened in 1947 it became the first postwar gold mine in the province. A community grew up around the mine site with up to 1,000 people. Renabie settled down to the business of hardrock mining for many years. A labour shortage closed the plant in 1970 and most people moved away, many to Missinabie. Over the next ten years there were several owners. One, Rengold Mines, actually put a producing gold mine into bankruptcy.

American Barrick and International Corona came to the rescue, putting the mine on a sound financial footing. A modernization program began and mill capacity was brought up to 700 tons a day. Under better management Renabie reached its one-million-ounce milestone in May 1989. Increased tonnage had been obtained by abandoning longhole stoping in favour of mining at depth with trackless sub-level caving. This improved mine safety, since miners no longer had to work in the stope. Backfill was gained from waste rock in the stope walls. A newly instituted production bonus was popular, but work became more difficult as mining went deeper. Ore had to be hauled up a winze, then taken 760 metres by battery-driven locomotives to the main shaft. At the time of the 1989 celebrations, it was estimated that the mine would have eight more years of operation, with the possibility of even longer life ince the orebody was open at depth. Management agreed that since the plant was in an isolated location it was responsible to a large degree for the welfare of the local community as well as its own 175 employees.

The Renabie Mine had a record year in 1990. An output of 48,000 ounces was the best in its history. Grade had dropped to 0.199 and direct operating costs were high — $359 for every ounce of the precious metal recovered. According to estimates, there were 1.2 million tons in reserve. Then a terse note in the 1990 annual report sounded the end for Renabie. Exploration at depth had found the widths and ore grade pinched off at depth — the mine was just not economical to work. Faced with only a quarter of the reserves estimated a year earlier, the owners made a decision to close the mine in September 1991. Decommissioning and severance costs were estimated at $4 million, and employees began looking for new jobs. At a handsome life-span production of 1.1 million ounces, Renabie had made a good profit for its investors.

Mining action in the Wawa area now centres around Goudreau and to the west. The Kremzar and Magnacon mines are closed but could resume working again when the price of gold picks up. Both have good reserves, and the Magnacon's mill has been eyed as a useful acquisition by other players in the area. One new development not far from Goudreau is the Spirit Lake Explorations work on the old Edwards property. High-grade has been found in the porphyry and mineralized carbonate zones. Hemlo Gold and Central Crude outlined a good deal of ore to the west in the English River project. They did underground development via a decline ramp, and the grade appears to be at least a quarter ounce of gold to the ton. Hemlo Gold was reluctant to proceed given current economic conditions, and its former partner obtained the property, selling it to Western Quebec Mines. More than two million tons rated at quarter of an ounce to the ton have been outlined. The property, 50 kilometres west of Wawa, will likely make a profitable mine.

Gold is also scattered around Sudbury, but the area is too big to be defined as a gold camp. One producing gold mine was the New Gold Rose. The hard-luck plant is reported to have lost money every year of its 1937–44 life. Other mines that operated were Shakespeare, Crystal, High Crow, Spanish River, Bousquet and Macmillan. The only producer of any significance, the Long Lake (or Lebel Ora), gave up more than 50, 000 ounces. Most of the Sudbury-area gold deposits were of high grade. This still spurs prospectors on as they fan out in the bush. Nickel is the dominant metal in the Sudbury basin, but both Inco and Falconbridge produce gold as a by-product of base-metal mining. There are also several locations where placer gold has been discovered. A low grade has hindered development, but nuggets have occasionally been found and this encourages people to look for the mother lode.

The Associated Goldfields Mine at "Larder Lake City" in 1924. The mine is long-gone, but the small town of Larder Lake remains — a city never did materialize. – PA 13646

Australian-born prospector Jack Costello outside his cabin near Larder Lake (March 12, 1933). The place was built small to discourage visitors who might slow his work. Costello found two properties but never made money on them. – MNR

Jack Davidson (second from left) with his camp crew at Larder Lake. He prospected all across Canada and is best known for his Matachewan discovery, which became the Young Davidson Mine. – OA 741

LARDER LAKE

I have often been asked: "What do you know of Larder Lake?" I have to answer: "I don't know anything and I haven't yet found a man who does."

ANSON GARD, ROVING JOURNALIST, 1909

THE KIRKLAND LAKE GOLD CAMP followed the Porcupine in production start-up, but another gold area close by was discovered first. The Larder Lake area, which includes the ground from Dobie through to Virginiatown, was first host to prospectors in 1906. University of Toronto geologist W.A. Parks visited the area briefly in 1904 after working in the booming Cobalt silver fields. His assistant, H.L. Kerr, paid attention when he was told the area warranted a more thorough investigation. Two years later, Kerr (then manager of the University Mine in Cobalt), revisited the northwest arm of Larder Lake with Bill Addison. They found that Robert Reddick had already staked claims, so they took ground near his property. Reddick managed to bring a mine into production with such notables on his board as Sam Hughes (later Canada's militia minister) and Sir Frederick Borden. Between 1907 and 1911, some $314 worth of ore was mined from a shallow shaft in the tiny mine. Gold from this ore was eventually used in the first $5 gold piece minted in Canada. Meanwhile Kerr sold his claims to Canadian Associated Goldfields, which also picked up the Reddick property.

The small success at Reddick's claims sparked a gold rush to Larder Lake. From 1906 to 1910 forty companies had interests in the vicinity. At first they were attracted by showings of coarse visible gold. Trenching and small shafts revealed narrow, high-grade quartz veins in silicified dolomite. A great deal of money was spent by the mining companies, and the main camp was dignified with the name Larder City. But by 1910 it was generally realized that such small isolated gold occurrences would not support mines and the camp dissolved. Larder City was left a few empty buildings and tent frames. Over the next decade the mine centred in the Reddick and Kerr Addison claims was worked fitfully but finally abandoned in 1922. That was a shame — the same ground would eventually become the site of one of the richest mines in Canada.

Despite the decline of Larder City there was still some mining action in the area. In 1912 gold was discovered in Gauthier Township on the west shore of Beaverhouse Lake. The property was developed by La Mine d'Or Huronia and then became the Argonaut Mine, working intermittently under various names until 1922. A 200-ton mill was erected, and by the time the place first closed in

1928, it had become the first mine to make a profit in the Larder Lake camp, having produced $800,000 in gold, silver and copper. Just after this property was discovered, an Australian prospector, Jack Costello, found gold at Pancake Lake just east of the present Larder Lake Station. He returned in 1919 after war service to find his claims intact, since assessment work was waived during the conflict. Jack worked alone and lived in a tiny one-man cabin to discourage visitors who might arrive and slow down his efforts. His claims were eventually purchased and found their way into the Canadian Associated Goldfields treasury. The prospector was not happy with the $6,000 he split with a former backer, so he passed a hint to an employee of Cobalt's Crown Reserve Mine that ground lay open next to the Associated property. The vacant ground was staked, and despite urging by the Associated manager, George Grey, no attempt was made by that firm to obtain the claims from the Cobalt company.

Mine watchers were treated to a spectacle rare in the industry as the two rival companies sank shafts barely 90 metres apart, essentially working the same vein. Associated won the race and built a small mill, recovering $52,295 in gold and silver. Crown Reserve had little success underground and never erected a mill. Associated was now being called Canadian Assassinated by local wags. It lived up to this new tag by going bankrupt. Both firms closed in 1928 after having sunk their shafts below 300 metres. For the next eight years, various schemes were tried to bail them out. Finally Jack Bickell of the McIntyre put up the money to place the properties on a sound footing, and they were joined as Jack Costello had always recommended. The place operated as Omega Gold Mines from 1936 to 1947. By the time it closed, 29,290 ounces had been produced at a 0.13 grade — marginal for the period. As for Costello, he kept on prospecting but never found enough for another mine and lived out his life at Larder Lake in near poverty.

Thirty years after the first discoveries of gold at Larder Lake, the Rip Van Winkle of mining camps finally awoke. Just west of the old Reddick claims was ground originally staked in 1907 by J.T. Kearns (a village is named after him). Although what became known as the Chesterfield Gold Mines acquired other claims, one held ore and was destined to be the only giant mine in the camp. The Chesterfield property, divided by Highway 66, had been dormant since its discovery. In 1937 diamond drilling outlined more than a million tons of ore. From 1938 until it closed in 1952, the Chesterfield produced continuously. Twenty levels were mined from its 854-metre shaft. The 500-ton mill delivered a handsome 458,880 ounces of low 0.11-grade gold.

The ten Kerr Addison and Reddick claims were acquired from Proprietory Mines in 1930 but nothing was accomplished until 1936. Then, George Webster, who had promoted the revival of the Omega, managed to convince Proprietory and other original investors from the old Associated company to participate in what became Kerr Addison Gold Mines. Initial funds raised allowed the firm to buy a small pilot plant. The dolomite in the ridge that had drawn the original stakers 30 years earlier was carefully sampled. Four parallel tunnels spaced at 120-metre intervals were driven into the hillside. Initial results were disappointing, but the old shaft on the property was pumped out and underground drilling came up with two new orebodies missed in previous exploration. With such good news, the Imperial Bank of Commerce was persuaded to provide start-up funds of

Upper Canada number 1 headframe (1941). – Queenston

$250,000, an unusual move, as banks of the period did not usually back risky propositions such as gold mines. Production commenced in 1938, and the 500-ton mill was expanded to 1,200 within a year.

The Kerr Addison began rewarding patient investors, and during the same period Upper Canada Mines was organized in Gauthier Township. The village of Dobie grew up to house the miners. The Upper Canada ground lies within Temiskaming sediments, volcanics and pyroplastics. Vein zones dipped vertically, with the strongest ore structure running to the deepest levels at 1,612 metres. Over the years adjacent properties were purchased until the mine held forty-six claims. Up to the 1971 closing, 4,648,984 ounces of 0.30-grade gold were produced. In 1964 Upper Canada purchased the Lake Beaverhouse Mine and changed the name to Upper Beaver, operating the property until 1972. The smaller mine, which had four different names in its existence, had a lifetime output of 580,562 ounces of 0.24-grade gold. Although the parent Upper Canada Mine was closed, its mill was kept in good order and the facility was used later.

A townsite called Virginiatown was constructed to house employees of Kerr Addison, and after the war another subdivision, North Virginiatown, was built to meet increased demands for living accommodation as more employees settled in the area. In addition, bunkhouses for 400 men were built to be used during the various construction periods. The new town provided churches, stores, a curling club and even a theatre. Although the work force was depleted during the war years, by 1959 there were 1,456 people employed at the big mine. The mill expanded in 1948 to 4,500 tons per day. The company was debt free and for many years paid eighty percent of its earnings in dividends. Kerr Addison entered the fifties with reserves of 16.7 million tons of ore. From 1957 to 1961 more than half a million ounces of gold were produced annually. In 1960 the mine that had taken 30 years to get started produced more gold than any other mine in the Western hemisphere.

In 1936 the Kerr Addison Mine near Virginiatown was just an adit in the rock. The mine would later become one of the world's largest gold mines. – PA 17721

No mine can stand such a high production rate for long. Production declined steadily from 1962, though earnings remained high well into the seventies due to the increase in the price of gold. The industry prediction was that the mine would close by 1980. But on April 14, 1982, a bar was poured containing the ten-millionth ounce. To that time only the Homestake (in South Dakota), the Hollinger, the McIntyre and the Dome had exceeded that level. By 1984 the work force had dropped to 329 and only 47,211 ounces were shipped. Since its opening, the mine had delivered $581.8 million in bullion and given dividends of $166 million.

West of Larder Lake the bush always echoes to the clatter of diamond drills. The old Upper Beaver Mine has been the object of much activity in the past few years. Pamorex initiated exploration work in the late eighties, and then Queenston and Royal Oak took over. A combination of gold and copper finds (one of which is below the old workings) grades at 0.16. The mill at the long-closed Upper Canada Mine came in handy when the McBean Mine, a nearby open-pit property, operated between 1984 and 1986. The grade of 0.08 was very low, but the method of extraction and adjacent mill made the project viable with a recovery of 45,900 ounces. Exploration work on the Upper Canada and adjacent Pawnee property have indicated sizable reserves. To the west, the Anoki project held by Queenston and Inco is considered a certain producer. The only snag is that gold would have to climb considerably in price before it would be worthwhile to go underground. Sudbury Contact does not have that problem at its nearby Victoria Creek property. It is confirming a large low-grade orebody, and the area bush is now a hive of exploration activity.

The Kerr Addison Mine, once one of the great elephants of Canadian mining, had its darkest days in 1988. A year earlier, the mine had been acquired by an over-ambitious junior mining company. Within a year the former 10.25-million-ounce producer was in bankruptcy. The mine was acquired by Deak Resources, which aggressively sought financing from both government and private sources. Citizens

By 1956 Kerr Addison was processing 4,500 tons a day. – Deak Resources

of Virginiatown, home to many mine employees, watched the developments anxiously, for the town had no other industry. By May 1990 the mine (renamed the Kerr Mine) was working again. The mill circuit was updated and enlarged, modified to take custom milling in addition to its own ore. Since that time several small mines have had their product trucked to the big mill for processing. On its own account the venerable mine produced 15,350 ounces of 0.053-grade gold in 1993. Exploration continued and higher-grade reserves were found.

Once the Kerr was milling gold again, the owners signed various agreements with other companies for joint explorations in the vicinity. The adjacent Chesterfield property was one of the prime targets. Later, the A. J. Perron Company took over the Kerr Mine from Deak. The mine produced 22,000 ounces in 1994 and will likely more than double that figure in 1995. Two other small mines within the shadow of the Kerr headframe have also been active. Armistice Resources put up a headframe on an old forties-era shaft near Barber Lake and deepened the former workings. Drilling was done to connect with the Kerr orebody, and after a brief closure, the property is being examined and the potential orebody enlarged by exploration drilling. Not far west from the red Armistice shafthouse, Northfield Minerals' Cheminis Mine also sits on the Larder Lake break. Unlike the neighbouring mine, the Cheminis is in production. A 589-ounce bar was poured in November 1991, and 1,200 ounces of 0.13-grade gold were milled by year-end. In 1994 the small property produced 6,254 ounces of gold.

Over at the Kerr Mine, local sculptors have joined to pay tribute to the mine's contribution to the area with a sculpture that portrays different aspects of hardrock mining. Set in a slender column are familiar tools of the trade — an axe, tongs, a hard hat, a shovel and goggles. Many junior companies doing exploration work in the Larder Lake area are confident that the demand for gold will soon be matched by adequate compensation in the marketplace.

37

The big number 11 headframe at the McIntyre Mine was completed in 1927. Older shafthouses were still in place. – Author collection

The Hollinger Mine was one of the largest gold producers in the world when this picture was taken in 1935.
– PA 17666

GOLD IN THE PORCUPINE

Gold up in Porcupine, everybody knows.

THE PORCUPINE SONG

THE FIRST MAN to come across gold in the Porcupine was Reuben D'Aigle. After moderate success in placer mining in Alaska, he saved money to bankroll future trips and went back to school. D'Aigle knew he had much to learn, and Queen's University at Kingston offered a two-week course on minerals. While there he read survey reports of gold traces in the Porcupine country of Northeastern Ontario. He financed two trips to the area, working his way by the water route from the CPR line west of Sudbury. The numerous rock outcroppings looked promising to the prospector. On the second trip he staked several claims and took samples but left depressed by the amount of quartz he saw. For him, the presence of quartz overshadowed any visible gold. He never did register his claims, because none of the Porcupine showings seemed spectacular enough to make a mine. This was a shame, since the pits and hand-steel he left behind turned out to be at the centre of a fortune in precious metal. D'Aigle moved on and was involved at the start of another promising camp in Quebec, but he never did hit the big time.

Gold was reported in the Porcupine between 1899 and 1903 by provincial surveyors and geologists. The Lake of the Woods rush had proved disappointing. It was inevitable that prospectors would move east across Northern Ontario. Victor Mattson and Henry Banella had the first mine in the Nighthawk Lake area. They worked it in 1907 and produced one small gold bar from a crude mill before fire put them out of business. They were followed by George Bannerman and Tom Geddes. North of Porcupine the partners found good surface showings, and their samples caused much excitement when they went to record their claims. The result was the Scottish–Ontario Mine (later named the Canusa and the Banner Porcupine).

The three great properties that formed the anchor for the Timmins–Porcupine gold camp were all found in the summer of 1909. The first was staked by Jack Wilson, a long-time prospector who believed in big exploration crews to even the odds against discovery. His eight-man party left the Temiskaming & Northern Ontario Railway line near Driftwood (now Monteith) and worked the way to the Porcupine by portage and paddle. After two weeks a large quartz outcrop caught their attention. Wilson noticed free gold, and by evening the excited crew had chipped off high-grade specimens from a big vein, which later became known as the Golden

Staircase for the spongelike blobs found stepping down along its path. Financing of promising properties went quickly in those days. One of Wilson's Chicago-based backers accompanied him to the discovery site as soon as the claims were registered, and the deal was made around a campfire.

Benny Hollinger was a barber in Haileybury and Alec Gillies cut firewood while they rustled up enough money to stake prospecting trips. The partners left for the Porcupine after hearing about the Bannerman discoveries but found Wilson's party had taken all the ground in the vicinity of the big quartz dome. They pushed on 6 kilometres to the west and came across Reuben D'Aigle's rusting drill steel lying in the pits he had blasted the previous year. The boys felt the place was worthwhile investigating if someone else had spent so much time and effort there. They split up and shortly after, Benny yell brought his partner rushing to his side. Hollinger had been pulling moss off rocks and uncovered quartz with gold splattered through it about 2 metres wide by 18 metres along the vein. For the next few hours the happy pair did not rest but continued staking, mindful of other prospectors who could be right behind them.

A party of three had indeed heard their jubilant cries. A good gold strike could be the only cause for excitement in that lonely bush country. Clary Dixon, Tom Middleton and Jack Miller saw the young prospectors from Haileybury and moved off to secure open land to the west. Two other men came up at this time and quickly sized up the situation. Newly teamed partners Hans Buttner and Sandy McIntyre headed north. They figured there was no sense staying in a place where ground was already taken and felt that gold might be found near the original claims. The two latecomers took their land on Pearl Lake, which would become the McIntyre, the third great mine in the camp. They went out to record their claims but then split up, only meeting back in the camp four years later to be photographed in the location they had staked their claims. As for Miller, Dixon and Middleton, parts of their claims were picked up by the Hollinger Mine, while others became the basis of the Middleton and Coniaurum mines.

By October 1909 the richest ground was taken as the Porcupine gold rush came into its own. Golden City (now Porcupine) was the first settlement. Next came Pottsville, which soon joined up with South Porcupine. The town of Timmins, an initial Hollinger venture, was not laid out until 1912. Several mines found in the first five years became producers or were amalgamated with others. These included the Mace, Vipond, Coniaurum, Anglo–Huronian, Acme, Pearl, Newray, West Dome, Porcupine Crown and Carium mines. The area has never been without a producing gold mine since 1911. It has since been found that the gold-producing area is 5 kilometres wide and 8 kilometres long. Transportation to the new camp was difficult after supplies and passengers left the T&NO northbound line for the trek into the Porcupine. Such was the potential of the Dome, the Hollinger and the McIntyre that within two years of discovery a rail link was made between Timmins and the main line.

The Dome was the first of these mines to come into production, and the Timmins family secured the Hollinger ground. Noah and Henry Timmins had made their money in the Cobalt silver camp, and their nephew, mining engineer Alphonse Pare, was sent on a fact-finding trip to determine the strength of the

Noah Timmins's son, Jules, stamps a gold bar at the Hollinger in the early sixties. The big mine closed soon after. – Mines Library

McIntyre Mine owner J.P. Bickell supported the Banting Institute in silicosis research and also helped finance Maple Leaf Gardens in Toronto. – OA S381

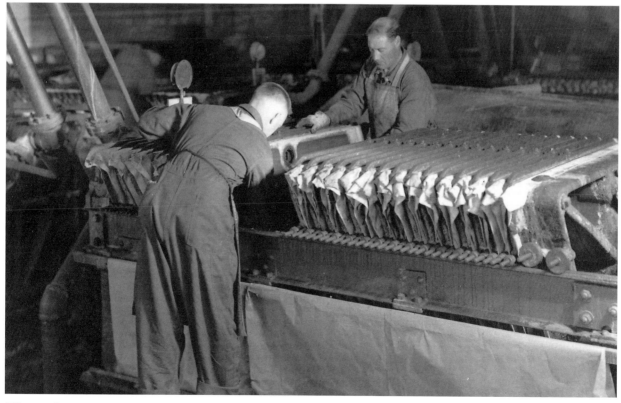

These refinery workers are scraping black zinc and gold precipitate from filter cloths (Hollinger Mine, October 1936). – PA 17544

Joseph Noseworthy operating a mucking machine at the McIntyre Mine (1916). – PA 122372

Miners operating an Ingersoll Rand drill in the Schumacher Mine. – PA 17437

Hollinger claims. His accounts of their riches were so glowing that his uncles, trusting their nephew's judgement, bought the claims and thus guaranteed the family fortune. By contrast, the McIntyre Mine was slow to finance. Even after its 1912 incorporation, the mine was shaky for the first few years. Actually the "Mac" was fortunate in its slow development. Many other properties were devastated in the great 1911 fire, which laid waste much of the new gold camp. Thousands of claim posts were destroyed, leaving a headache for the mining recorder, as ownership had to be confirmed and properties relocated. Prospectors hit the bush right after the disaster, figuring that the rush of wind and flames would have stripped some ground and laid promising veins open to view.

The Porcupine settled down to the life of a hardrock mining camp once the initial surface gold had been quarried off. Several small mines had to close after the fire, but the Dome built a big surface plant to replace the one lost in the flames. The three big mines consolidated by taking over adjacent properties. The Dome added the Dome Extension, the Hollinger took over the Acme and the Middleton, while the McIntyre, at last on a firm footing, acquired the Jupiter, McIntyre Extension, Pearl Lake and later the Plenarium and Platt Vet properties. The Hollinger absorbed the Schumacher Mine, which closed in 1918. In its four-year life, 27,182 ounces of 0.24-grade gold were produced. Millionaire philanthropist Fred Schumacher maintained a presence in the camp, contributing his name to the community, buying and selling properties, and even donating Christmas toys for children — a practice his estate has continued to the present.

Any gold camp has small mines that produce steadily with unspectacular results. The Davidson Mine opened in 1918. The small Tisdale Township producer worked for two years. The Reef, a steady mine with 0.23-grade gold, worked for 51 years. The Vipond in Tisdale opened in 1911, the year the camp really began producing, but was mined out in 1941. One small mine, the West Dome, was the scene of a tragedy during the 1911 fire. Many people were killed, including manager Bob Weiss and his family. They all died of asphyxiation while taking shelter in the shaft. That West Dome property became part of the new Paymaster Mine in 1966.

Sandy McIntyre was involved in two other gold camps but made money with only one of them. Money trickled through his fingers and he lived out his last years on a pension from the mine he had discovered. Benny Hollinger lost his stake through ill-advised speculative ventures. Barney McEnany, for whom Hollinger had staked a claim that later sold for half a million dollars, bought his old friend a house in Pembroke. Hollinger spent his last years there. The camp both men had helped to spark was so rich in gold that, except for a slump in the sixties and seventies, new mines have opened there in every decade since.

As public confidence returned after the war, prospectors went back to work and promising ground opened for mining. The Cincinnati Mine was so named to attract American investors but gave up only 736 ounces from 1922 to 1924. The Banner, George Bannerman's old Scottish–Ontario Mine, was worked from 1928 to 1929 and again from 1933 to 1935. The owners stuck with the small mine, for though in its life it gave up only 670 ounces, they were a rich 2.13 ounces to the ton. The Porcupine Peninsular worked from 1924 to 1941, and the Ankerite ran from 1926 to 1935. With a total production of 61,039 ounces in that period, the Ankerite delivered what one medium-size gold mine would deliver annually today. Gillies Lake is now a recreational spot, but the long-vanished mine of the same name gave up 15,000 ounces from 1929 to 1937.

The second mine named Ankerite was in Deloro Township and produced close to a million ounces in its long run, from 1926 to 1953. The Hugh Pam opened the same year but closed due to technical and financial problems. The place did not reopen until 1948 but produced gold until 1965. The Coniaurum was the biggest mine to open in the twenties. It operated from 1928 to 1961 and milled 1,109,574 ounces at a 0.25 grade. The Hollinger Company was now so wealthy that it was able to bankroll the start-up of Noranda Mines to the tune of $3 million. The Hollinger was the biggest gold mine in the British Empire, but its success did not prevent tragedy. On February 10, 1928, there were 920 men underground when a fire broke out. Thirty-nine never made it to the surface. These men died despite the efforts of local miners and the men who came by relief trains from Toronto and Pennsylvania. The legislative result was that mine rescue stations were set up in all the mining camps — Timmins opened the first one in 1929. In the same year, a fire destroyed the mill at the Dome. A cleanup of the machinery and ashes netted $500,000 in bullion, unexpectedly providing much of the reconstruction costs.

The thirties hosted the lost years of the Depression, but in the Porcupine area the economic downturn was not felt as widely as in other parts of the country. Fourteen new gold producers opened in that trying decade. The McLaren, Kingsbridge (or Gomak), Halcrow–Sawyze and Concordia mines all went bust, mining less than 100 ounces each. The Porcupine Lake (or Hunter) never paid for its own plant, with only 1,369 ounces recovered. The output of the tiny Tionaga Mine was never recorded, but its 0.39 grade must have kept the investors happy for a while.

A Marcy rod mill made by Atlas Steel photographed just after it was delivered to the Hollinger Mine in 1929. – PA 15574

Only two of the smaller mines lasted. The De Santis and Naybob were in Ogden Township. Opening in 1937, the De Santis produced 35,842 ounces in three separate incarnations totalling 27 years. The Naybob ran non-stop from 1932 to 1964 and returned a modest 50,731 ounces.

Timmins celebrated its quarter century in 1937 and evidence of prosperity was all around. Six mines opened in the recovery years of that decade and were big producers. The Preston East Dome in Tisdale Township was finally brought into production by promoter Joe Hirshorn. Overshadowing its three tiny associated mines, New York, Porcupine Pete and Porcupine Hill, the Preston rewarded investors with 1,539,355 ounces before it closed in 1968. In Whitney Township, the Broulan Reef Mine extracted a quarter of a million ounces during its 1937–64 operating life. The Moneta Mine, a small property standing between the Hollinger and the streets of Timmins, capitalized on the Hollinger veins, which ran into its ground. The mine produced 149,250 ounces of 0.47-grade gold before closing in 1943. The plant is gone now but has lent its name to part of the city. The Halnor Mine put together the former Porcupine Creek and Poulet Vet properties and returned 1,645,892 ounces before it closed in 1968. The most noteworthy of all the mines that added to the Porcupine skyline in the thirties was the Pamour. The plant made a success of three small earlier mines. Still running despite a 0.11 grade, the Pamour has produced more than 3.5 million ounces. The present owners, Royal Oak, should profit from the mine for many years to come.

The Second World War brought a slowdown to all gold mining camps. The Vipond and Moneta closed, but six smaller mines opened and one large property started that would have a 44-year life. Mainly low-grade operations that lasted from two to six years, the Faymar, Fuller, Hoyle and Jerome mines did their bit to keep the local economy healthy. The Bonetal ran from 1941 to 1951 and produced 51,510 ounces at a 0.15 grade. The Gold Hawk had two brief life-spans. In 1947 it lost money with only 47 ounces produced but gave it another try in 1980 and delivered a more encouraging 3,697 ounces. The Aunor Mine opened in 1940, demonstrating that the Deloro Township still had plenty of ore. As of its 1984 closure, 2,502,214 ounces of 0.30-grade gold had been recovered.

The original three great mines remained the mainstay of mining activity, but the next three decades saw little new in area gold-mining activity. Only two mines opened in the fifties. The Tisdale Ankerite milled just over 2,000 ounces when it operated in 1952. The Bonwhit was an excellent venture in its short 1951–54 life, delivering a good 0.30 grade for a total of 67,940 ounces. But the bright light on the horizon in the sixties was not gold. A huge copper-zinc find in Kidd Township meant many new jobs and a huge base-metal mine that would last into the next century. The timing was right as the great Hollinger Mine was forced to close in 1968. It had been in operation for as long as the town had been incorporated and contributed much to the social life of Timmins. One of the biggest mines in the world, it had produced more than 19 million ounces of gold. Several of its principal buildings still grace the city skyline, including a new headframe that could be operated again if the price of gold took a significant upward hike.

Still operating more than 80 years after it first opened, the Dome Mine is the longest-working gold mine in Canada. A lengthy strike in 1990 curtailed output. Following the strike, the company dealt with dramatically rising production costs by cutting its work force by half. The Dome also returned to open-pit mining — the method the mine started with in 1910 before going underground. The old Glory Hole Mine is being enlarged and reworked with technology from the Placer Dome mines. Results are so positive that the surface plant and townsite are being moved to make way for the pit operation. In 1994 they took 174,000 ounces of gold from the combined operation. The "super-pit" will cost $150 million to put into operation but should provide 25 more years of production — a boost of more than seventy percent. With the addition of close to a million tons of ore expected from the nearby Paymaster Mine, which is being brought back into operation, the Dome is expected to remain the oldest operating gold mine in Canada for a long time to come.

To the east, Pamour Mine prospers under Royal Oak control. President Margaret Witte has merged companies in the Porcupine and Yellowknife to form an aggressive exploration-oriented firm. As well as Pamour, Royal Oak has interests in former producers all along the camp, including the Delnite, Schumacher, Ross, Coniaurum and Broulan mines. All have mineable reserves, and since the mines under this Vancouver-based firm's control have produced more than 41 million ounces since incorporation, the bet is that they will deliver many more. Pamour itself has been the lowest production-cost gold mine in the country for some time. This has been achieved despite a generally low grade of ore. From two open pits and the underground operation, the venture gave up 90,000 ounces of gold in 1994. The ore from the Hoyle property across the other side of Highway 101 is brought to surface via the Pamour shaft. The highway itself was relocated some time ago at the mine's expense so that the open pit could be enlarged. The company is also dewatering the former Hallnor Mine to access ore left behind when it closed in 1981. Royal Oak is shaving costs in all its properties by using bulk tonnage and extraction methods while working out ways of mining high-grade narrow veins economically. By 1995, the Night Hawk Lake gold property was accessing ore via a ramp. The ground beneath the huge lake will once more give up gold, as it did in the earliest days of the Porcupine camp.

The Detour Lake Mine is a large-scale modern operation north of Cochrane in isolated country 5 kilometres from the Quebec border. The mineral prospects were detected long before prospectors walked the ground. An airborne geophysical survey identified an anomaly as a potential target. In 1974 diamond drilling proved it to be a major deposit located in quartz veins in a volcanic complex. Open-pit production began with the first gold coming from the mill in 1983. The total cost of the mine, including an initial bush road driven through from Paradis, Quebec, the pit (which closed in 1987) and the complete surface and underground plant, came to $139 million. Just when some of the huge initial investment began to be recouped, the ore grade dropped and equipment problems were experienced. The whole operation had to be reexamined for economic viability in every area. The 2,400-ton mill delivers around 124,000 ounces of gold annually and will soon go to 200,000 ounces, with diamond drilling having extended ore reserves. The work force is smaller than in the heady days of $800 U.S. per ounce, but one innovation has benefited Native people. The Nishnawbe–Aski nation is providing about nine percent of the work force. The work is welcome in an area of high unemployment.

Motorists travelling west to Timmins can see the blue-steel St. Andrews Goldfields shafthouse in Stock Township just off Highway 101. The structure looks new and yet the development and its headframe have been working since 1974. Several properties had to be acquired before underground work commenced. The mine sits on the Porcupine–Destor Fault and has produced since 1989. Since that time the fault has been responsible for ground control problems. Ore comes to surface part way via an internal ramp. Rock bolting underground maintains stability and for every 8 metres mined, a rock pillar is left. Working up to 700 tons per day, the mill has treated ore from the Goldpost property in Hislop Township and other locations near the mine. Reserves are not great, so extraction costs are a prime consideration in this 0.15-grade mine. The mine recovered 23,788 ounces in 1993 but closed in 1994 to refinance the enterprise for more exploration.

The volatile nature of gold prices in recent years soon scuttled the Bell Creek Mine, the flagship of Canamax Resources. Using flow-through financing, the firm opened five mines from 1985 to 1990. The one at Bell Creek, just west of the Kidd Creek metallurgical plant, went into production in 1987 and closed four years later. Gold production costs were $350 an ounce and the price of the precious metal was dropping below that figure. Kinross Gold bought the property and gained 6,695 ounces in 1994 with its new 425-ton mill. The new owner will use the mill to run its feed from the Hoyle Pond Mine and join it with the Bell Creek Mine by road. A healthy 55,000 ounces was recovered from the Hoyle Pond Mine in 1994. Any further output there will be good news to the trustees of the Schumacher Estate, as the mine sits on their ground and royalties are paid on output.

Looking east to the Owl Creek open pit (foreground), mid-collar of the Hoyle Pond decline (centre), and Kidd Creek Metallurgical site (background). – Ed Spehar

A prominent staker in the Timmins area recently has been McKinnon Prospecting, the company run by Don McKinnon of Hemlo fame. One of his prospects is 6 kilometres northwest of Hearst in a belt 80 kilometres by 3 kilometres roughly parallel to Highway 11. McKinnon no longer has to scrounge for exploration dollars. He financed the extensive helicopter-aided geophysical survey of this area using earnings from his Hemlo royalties. Diamond drilling on the property was arranged by a company controlled by promoter Murray Pezim, another Hemlo veteran. The ground at Hurdman Township has produced gold, silver, zinc and copper showings. The Kidd Creek smelter would be a prime candidate for the ore if the property pans out. As for Don McKinnon, it would gratify him to see much-needed jobs created in the now economically depressed area where he spent most of his life.

The Porcupine camp is always in the news. Mine promoter Viola MacMillan made a great deal of money there. In 1990 she donated $1.2 million of it toward the establishment of a mineral collection to be housed in a gallery named for her at the Museum of Natural Science in Ottawa. The underground-mine tour at the old Hollinger Mine draws visitors from across the continent, but this gold camp is not relegated to history. Mining is still a mainstay of Timmins. The area has not been without an operating gold mine since 1910, and many more gold-bearing locations remain to be developed. One company, Timginn Syndicate, is even drilling for the precious metal within city limits.

The giant surface hoist of the Lake Shore Mine in the 1930s.   – OA 9465

*A rare view of a horse-drawn whim in action
(the Continental Kirkland Mine, 1932).*

– Author collection

*The assay office of the Teck Hughes Mine (1927)
survives today and is considered a prime example
of good industrial architecture.*   – OA 9465

THE TOWN THAT STANDS ON GOLD

Gold has a mind of its own...
gold is a woman.

ROSA BROWN

FIRST BUILT as a development road, the T&NO Railway fulfilled its mandate once silver was discovered at Cobalt. Prospectors made their way ahead of the rails to Larder Lake. Some continued west, catching up with the line that was being constructed toward Cochrane. Claims were staked along the way but almost all lapsed for want of assayers. The spot where these prospectors boarded the train was first called Bell's Siding. Gold was seen in the vicinity, along the tracks, and by 1908 there were two small mines separated by the railway and a creek. The one west of the line near Otto Lake was called the Swastika (later the Crescent Mine); the other was named the Lucky Cross. They were eventually joined as Gateford Mines, which through many openings and closings to 1947, produced 30,068 ounces of 0.29-grade gold. Eventually the village that served both the railway and the mines was named Swastika.

The country east of Swastika was mapped by provincial surveyor L.V. Rorke. He came across a handsome lake and called it Kirkland Lake (after his secretary, Winifred Kirkland). During 1909 and 1910 most prospectors bypassed Swastika on their way to the Porcupine gold rush. Few found the elusive metal they sought. Harry Oakes was different. He was a wanderer who had worked in gold camps around the world. He had seen a map showing the area north of North Bay and wondered if there was promising ground between the mineral areas of Cobalt and the Porcupine. He stopped off at Swastika and met Rosa Brown, a cook and prospector who encouraged him to try the area around Kirkland Lake.

Swastika became a staging point and home base for goldseekers. The two original mines were fragile enterprises, so the newcomers looked elsewhere for prospects. Fifty prospectors eventually staked the ground that would contain the big mines, but only two earned a big return for their efforts. George Minaker was a teamster who left his haulage work long enough to take three claims near Kirkland Lake on February 23, 1911. The most northerly would later be among the richest mines in Canada, but by then Minaker was back working in the bush.

Bill Wright and his partner, brother-in-law Ed Hargreaves, found the first free gold in reddish feldspar porphyry on July 27, 1911. The men were so hard up that

The Tough–Oakes–Burnside Mine, shown here in 1926 with its mill and aerial tramway, would soon close and reopen as the Toburn Mine. – PA 13867

Hargreaves had to go south to borrow the registration fee. In a few days' work the claims forming the basis for the Sylvanite and Wright–Hargreaves mines were staked. Hargreaves had a family to support and shortly after sold his share of the claims.

Swift Burnside soon staked three claims at the east end of the camp. Harry Oakes found five claims north of Burnside's group that would come open six months later since the owner had not done the necessary work to maintain its active status. He kept this knowledge to himself and, on the evening of January 8, 1912, approached railway contractors George and Jim Tough with a partnership offer. He would split profits with them if they would pay to register the claims they took. A deal was made and the trio set out at midnight in bitter-cold weather to snowshoe 6 kilometres to a location near Gull Lake. As it happened, Bill Wright showed up early the next morning, but by then the partners had set out their claims. The resulting Tough Oakes Mine turned out to have the richest surface gold in the camp. It had a short life, operating only from 1913 to 1918.

Claims staked by Stephen Orr and John Reamsbottom just to the west of Kirkland Lake were purchased by Jim Hughes, who had made money both in the Klondyke and Porcupine. He hired Sandy McIntyre, a veteran from the Timmins area, to prospect the ground. McIntyre may have been heavy drinker but he was also a superb bush man. He criss-crossed the claims and found some promising veins with visible gold. They appeared to line up with the Wright veins to the east. At different times in 1911, Ed Horne, A. Maracle and Jack Matchett staked claims just south of the Wright–Hargreaves property. These claims eventually became the Townsite Mine. It was a loser, but Horne would go on to greater things as the discoverer of Noranda. At the same time, C.A. McKane and Dave Elliot staked ground on the west of Hughes's property. Five years later this would become the Kirkland Lake Gold Mine. It took more than ten years before the place produced at all.

Harry Oakes built a greenhouse adjacent to the Lake Shore bunkhouse to provide fresh vegetables for miners. The bunkhouse remains today as a motel. – OA 734

The giant Lake Shore Mine with Kirkland Lake in the background (1936). – PA 17635

Although staked by Ed Horne of Noranda fame, the Townsite Mine (1936) never made money. The author was principal of a school on the site. Today the shaft is located under the school gymnasium. – PA 15539

By that time, Bob Jowsey, who had done well in the South Lorrain silver fields, had bought the property.

Harry Oakes was still prowling the area looking for his own mine. Unlike most prospectors who worked to stake claims for sale, Oakes wanted to find a mine that he could retain long enough to reap the benefits of the gold it produced. He wore out relatives and acquaintances in an endless search for funds. His share in the Tough Oakes Mine helped to finance his quest. He built four rough cabins in the area and never stopped working. The single-minded prospector explained his regime: "I was up every morning before daybreak and on the go all day. At night I would head for the nearest of the little camps, cook myself a bite of supper and fall asleep dog-tired. I worked hard, harder than a lot of those syndicated grubstaked prospectors think they have to today." When Oakes had some spare cash he bought Melville McDougall's claim near the lake. Then, in July 1912, he picked up two water claims that came open when the owner failed to work the property. He kept ownership of the three parcels to himself until he was able to buy Minaker's north claim. He then registered all four claims and named the property Lake Shore. Unfortunately for Oakes, prospector Fred Connell had staked a fractional claim within the area that he later sold to the company for a handsome sum. Bill Wright went one better. He had a fraction abutting Lake Shore on the water and parted with it for cash and a seat on the mine's board of directors.

Oakes worked his ground, hiring help according to his income. He was a hard man and lost friends easily in his obsession with his hard-won property. Neither Lake Shore nor the other fledgling mines could get much done during the First World War. The Teck Hughes Mine commenced operations in 1917 and Sandy McIntyre frittered away his cash bonus and share allowance. In 1918, when Oakes's mine was incorporated, it still had trouble raising money. Power was difficult to maintain. It came from Charlton, 42 kilometres away and was sometimes cut off when the little generating station's capacity was overloaded. The new mines limped along and had a much slower start than the Porcupine. As for the Elliot claims at the west end of the camp, exploration to a depth of 152 metres did not yield promising results.

It took the success of one mine to turn the tide for investment in Kirkland Lake. The Lake Shore drifted into high-grade ore and Harry Oakes's years of scrambling for money were over. After he arranged for an infusion of capital, the camp was on the map as far as money markets were concerned. The Wright–Hargreaves expanded its surface plant and mill, and both the Lake Shore and Teck Hughes began to pay dividends. In 1922 the Tough Oakes reopened as the Tough–Oakes–Burnside Mine. The plant closed in 1928 but started again three years later as the Toburn. The elegant headframe still graces the east-end skyline, but the mine closed in 1953 after having produced 570,659 ounces of 0.48-grade gold.

There was always a friendly rivalry between the Porcupine and Kirkland Lake gold camps. The Timmins area had more mines and the output was greater, but the seven Kirkland Lake producers averaged a much higher grade. In the cases of the Wright–Hargreaves and Lake Shore, Bill Wright and Harry Oakes had become rich men. Today Oakes's elegant home, the Chateau, remains as the town museum. Oakes had once remarked that the Kirkland Lake camp was the slowest to get started, and this was certainly true of the Kirkland Lake Gold Mine. It had a 488-metre shaft but output was disappointing. There was a turnaround when Joseph Tyrell became president. Tyrell, the great Canadian land explorer, who among other things, discovered the Alberta dinosaur fossils, made a career later in life as a mining consultant. His theory that the ore dipped sharply westward through Kirkland Lake was confirmed as fact in 1926 when the shaft reached 755 metres and intersected good ore zones. The mine on the hill produced until 1960, delivering 1,172,955 ounces of 0.37-grade gold.

The Kirkland Rand Mine in the south end of town commenced operations in 1922 and a large plant was built. Activity there took place on and off until 1956 under five different companies, but only 483 ounces of low-grade gold were ever produced. By contrast, the Sylvanite Mine (next to the Toburn) began production in 1927 and gave up 1,674,808 ounces of gold at one third of an ounce to the ton before closing in 1961.

The mines of Kirkland Lake worked continuously during the Depression and toward the end of the thirties had over 5,000 employees with an annual gold output of at least $50 million. The Macassa Mine, the last of seven great mines on what became known as the Mile of Gold, opened during this period. Mine manager Bob Bryce inherited the Macassa property in 1926. It had already had much time and money expended on it. The old Elliot claims had been slow to give up their treasure. Only when Bryce was allowed to drive west from the 755-metre level of the Kirkland Lake Gold Mine was the ore intersected and a shaft put down to make contact with the deep orebody. Much to the regret of Harry Oakes, who had stepped down from the presidency of the company due to its slow progress, Macassa proved to be a constant producer of 0.44-grade gold to the present.

The Macassa Mine works today as a result of the acquisition, by LAC Minerals, of properties to the west. One of the problems LAC faced was that the distance from the shaft near the mill to the working places underground was too great for miners to be able to walk and return each shift. A new shaft would speed this up, enable more production, and access new ore areas. In 1983 Dynatec Mining commenced sinking a new shaft that, when completed 36 months later, was 2,355 metres deep. The depth of the new Macassa number-three shaft is greater than the height of four CN Towers placed end on end. In 1988, a new $20-million, 1,250-ton-per-day mill was completed to provide a 500-ton milling operation with the balance reserved for the Lake Shore tailings project. The Macassa Mine poured its 3-millionth ounce in 1990. The mine has experienced several rock bursts annually, but by implementing cemented backfilling and computerized micro-seismic monitoring, these occurrences have been cut down to one "bump" a year. Even so, the rock fall in November 1993 killed two miners and shut down the property for almost half a year, cutting production to only 19,856 ounces in 1994.

American Barrick bought out LAC and production resumed for the largest gold company on the continent. In 1995, mining methods were changed to long-hole production to improve both safety and output at the 64-year-old mine and the property was purchased by Kinross Gold. The new owner continued to refurbish a former producing shaft, which means that access may be gained to old gold-rich workings. The Macassa is the longest-operating of the original Kirkland Lake mines and the only one still working.

Near King Kirkland, the Bidgood Consolidated Mine opened in 1933. It also worked the adjacent Moffat Hall property. The mine milled 160,184 ounces of 0.27-grade gold before it closed in 1951. Through the thirties the Lake Shore vied with the Hollinger for recognition as the biggest gold mine in Canada. Lake Shore's output averaged 2,325 tons daily compared to the 5,000-ton output of the Timmins giant. But whereas the Porcupine output paid $8.88 per ton, the Kirkland Lake mines averaged $17.47 a ton. Having discovered a great mine, brought it into production and retained a major part of its wealth, Oakes finally separated from administration of the Lake Shore in the mid-thirties. The successful goldseeker was murdered in the Bahamas in 1943. The town he had helped to found peaked in prosperity in 1939, but a bitter strike took place in 1941 and the mines began to decline. The Wright–Hargreaves closed in 1965. With 4,821,296 ounces of 0.49-grade gold recovered, it was the second-largest producer in Kirkland Lake. First place went to the Lake Shore, which closed the same year. Since the late fifties, both mines had come under the control of a promising new company, Little Long Lac. The Lake Shore produced 8,573,246 ounces of gold averaging half an ounce to the ton in its life span. The Teck Hughes lasted until 1968 and, at 3,709,007 ounces of 0.37-grade gold, was the third-largest producer in the camp. The skeleton of its south headframe remains, towering over a modern motel, and across the road the dry and the machine shop now serve as part of a funeral home.

After the big mines closed in the sixties, Kirkland Lake languished for a while with just one remaining gold producer and a host of memories to show for its earlier success. Unlike most of the other Ontario gold camps, where the mines were located outside of the community, those in the Kirkland Lake camp were spaced

The Kirkland Lake Gold Mine. – Monette Collection

out in a line right through the built-up area. In the early days, when the main thoroughfare was being built, the road metal was mistakenly taken from an ore pile instead of the waste-rock pile. As a result, the government road has been called the Mile of Gold for the mines along it. A large iron-ore deposit south of town rescued the economy in 1964. The Adams Mine gave much-needed employment, but local thinking still leaned toward gold. Exploration continued and intensified in the eighties as gold peaked above $800 U.S.

In the early eighties, LAC Minerals decided that the once-great Lake Shore Mine was worth another look. The office complex and shafthouse were long-gone, and a shopping mall had been built on the site of the old mill. But old maps showed that ore still remained in the mine. The crown pillar also remained (a crown pillar is an umbrella of rock left to provide a roof for a mine) and was rich with ore. The first idea was to take the ore by open-pit mining. The trouble was that the mine was covered with the Kirkland Lake Mine, filled with tailings, directly above it. Eventually it was decided to get at the ore by spiralling down via a ramp near the old incline shaft that was used to take timber and other supplies underground. There was a bonus in that the main shaft of the Lake Shore was still serviceable. Two and a half million dollars later a new headframe was in place, surface buildings were ready for use, and the inclined roadway was taking vehicles. In traditional mining, ore is taken from above. At Lake Shore, LAC took the ore in pockets wherever it was found. After each section was removed, the area was filled with concrete to guard against cave-ins in the old workings. The reincarnated Lake

Miners installing a newly charged battery into a Goodman locomotive at the 2950 level in the Lake Shore Mine, 1936. – PA 17565

Shore Mine was worked from 1982 to 1987. Later, another firm tried to use the plant to access former mine properties to the west, but there was weak ground and the idea did not work. Tourists who see the shafthouse behind the mall get the impression that it is the original Lake Shore Mine — the current one is actually much smaller.

A new method of gold recovery came to the veteran gold town in the early eighties. Eastmaque Gold Mines, a Vancouver-based firm, obtained the rights to much of the mine tailings that had been dumped in the north end of the lake in the early days. The early mills did not grind or float the sulphides, and as a result, a small quantity of gold was lost with every ton of discharged waste. From 1984 to 1987, the company prepared the ground, tested material, and gained zoning changes and environmental permits. A mill with a diversion channel for surface water was built on the former lake bed. Eastmaque would work year-round on the water despite only a hundred frost-free days a year and temperatures that fall to -35°C.

A dredge with a 16.8-metre ladder and an underwater pump took tailings on a 24-hour basis to a depth of 13.7 metres. Slurried tailings were pumped along several hundred metres of pipe to the mill, where debris from the old lake bed was screened out. Since the gold was not in hardrock form, half the regular mill processes could be omitted, making the process relatively inexpensive. The dried concentrate, with a grade of at least two ounces to the ton, was then trucked to a smelter in Noranda. Two of three dredges would work at a time in the 2,336-ton-per-day operation. Then in 1990, gold values dropped. By November 1991 the innovative plant had closed. Lower grades and falling gold prices had scuttled the recovery and left 15.5 million tons of gold-bearing tailings in the lake bed to await a more promising economic climate. True to its reclamation plan, Eastmaque

A crew of Dynatec shaft sinkers in the cage ready to descend into the Macassa Mine. – LAC

commenced a seven-year program of revegetating the tailings and making a new diversion channel to allow water to flow back to where it was before. When finished, the ground would be more attractive than in its former state. In all, 70,000 ounces of gold were recovered from a tailings-filled lake that people oblivious to the bonanza stored beneath their feet had walked over for years.

From the rear verandah of the Sir Harry Oakes Museum, visitors can watch a dredge working on the reclaimed Kirkland Lake and see a big black pipe snaking off 1.6 kilometres to the Macassa mill. Since 1989 the slimes have been pumped to the new facility. In 1993, the 750-ton-per-day circuit gave up 25,566 ounces of gold. The *Lady LAC* (a barge made in Mississippi) picks up gold-rich tailings. The operator moves his landlocked vessel to a new location by "spudding." This involves lifting the dredge ladder, swinging the vessel's front from side to side, and "walking" to a new location using the rear legs.

Queenston Mining is one of the most active junior companies in the camp. While gaining royalties from Macassa for production done on Queenston ground, the firm is involved in prospecting and drilling a large area with a break parallel to the famed fault that has provided gold in the area since 1912. In the former Amalgamated Kirkland property, Cyprus Canada has located a possible million-ounce deposit of 0.20-grade gold. Local mining people believe the place will be the first new producing gold mine in Kirkland Lake since 1933.

The Kirkland Lake gold camp has produced more than 24 million ounces of gold. Given the area's track record in large deposits of high-grade gold, exploration companies see the potential for more of the precious metal in the historic mining area.

Before it closed in 1918 the Miller Independence Mine produced 59 ounces of high-grade gold. – OA 6450-S8616

The Ashley Mine at Matachewan was the first good producer in that camp. It ran from 1932 to 1936. – MNR

The Matachewan Consolidated Gold Mine (1936). – PA 17632

A Small Golden Triangle

All you need to be a prospector is a strong back and a weak head.

FRED THOMPSON, PROSPECTOR

FOUR SMALL CAMPS in Northeastern Ontario fall within a golden triangle with a potential that has yet to be realized. In the order in which gold was first found, one point of the triangle is at Temagami, another at Boston Creek just south of Kirkland Lake, and the third is at Gogama and Shining Tree. The most successful camp to date within the triangle is at Matachewan.

Although gold was discovered in the Temagami area around the close of the nineteenth century, the district is better known for copper and iron. Parallel bands of greenstone are highly impregnated with iron pyrites. The sulphides contain at least enough gold to be valuable as a by-product and to keep bringing prospectors back for another look. So far, the best showings have been found in Strathy Township. Scores of properties have been examined there since 1904, but few have consistently held the interest of exploration managers.

Dan O'Connor was one of the most prominent business people in the early days of the Temagami settlement. In his time he was involved in hotels, boating and mining. His Big Dan Mine was located on the south shore of Net Lake and was active in 1904 when the plant burned. There were two shallow shafts and some 0.23-grade gold was recovered. Over the years the property has been worked several times with no significant results. The Little Dan, or Penrose, Mine at the west end of Arsenic Lake operated from 1904 to 1910; its main activity was in open cuts. The site was picked up again in the thirties with underground work financed by Bojo Mines but it was not considered profitable. Not far away, the Cominco property was staked by Paul Hermiston and R. McCauley in 1934. Much exploration has been done here, including a 115-metre shaft and considerable drifting. Published reports of visible gold have to be taken with a grain of salt, as the area has been dormant since the forties.

Inco and Falconbridge have base-metal interests in the Temagami area that are likely to contain gold, but a land caution obtained by the Teme–Augama Anishnaba Natives of Bear Island has restricted development. Recent activity in Strathy has been centred around what was known as the Beanland prospect. Explored by various companies since it was first staked and probed with a 153-metre shaft in

In 1936 there were several small mines in the Gogama–Shining Tree area. The Gomak Mine could only be reached by boat. – PA 15798

1929, the property is currently owned by Alex Perron and Gwen Resources, and the prospect is now known as Clenore. A bulk sample was taken from surface workings in 1992 for sampling at the Kerr Mill in Virginiatown. If the orebody has sufficient tonnage of the 0.28-grade ore thought to be present, Temagami could at last add gold to its historic base-metal output.

The Boston Creek gold camp has been a teaser for close to 75 years, yet the place keeps prospectors and risk capital coming back for more. From 1918 to 1987 probably two-thirds of the gold occurrences found were worked but only four are recorded as having shipped the precious metal. Most have changed ownership and names several times. The camp lies between the hamlet of Boston Creek and Highway 624, which runs from Englehart to Larder Lake. The lure of this area lies in visible gold scattered scattered at random over Boston, McElroy, Catherine and Skead townships. Unfortunately most of the gold occurrences are too small to be mined at a profit.

Geologist Willett Miller of Cobalt found gold in Boston Creek as early as 1900. The first claims were staked in 1906, sparked by the Larder Lake rush, and again in 1913 after the initial Kirkland Lake discoveries. The dominant formations are in Keewatin, where gold is found mainly in Algoman acid intrusives, often in dark streaks of chlorite and calcite. Boston Creek now boasts only seven occupied homes, but in the early days it was a thriving community that grew to serve the little mines that dotted the area. The only successful mine was the Barry–Hollinger. The name was an attempt to capitalize on the reputation of the famed discoverer of the great Hollinger Mine in Timmins. A forest fire wiped out the first plant in 1918 and the site lay dormant until work recommenced in 1925. In the early years, Barry–Hollinger shares went for twenty-five cents each in Canada, but because news was slow to reach the London market, the shares there were snapped up for sixty cents. The mine was worked until 1936 and then again from 1944 to 1946.

The Pacaud Township property had several surface veins but only one proved valuable underground. The ore was accessed by a winze to a depth of 668 metres. Over the life of the mine, 77,000 ounces of 0.20-grade gold were recovered.

Another Pacaud mine, the Miller Independence, was built on a claim staked in 1915 by Joe McDonough, a member of a great mining family. The little mine was trenched and had at least two shafts but it only operated in 1918. The rich 1.90-grade ore only gave up a total of 59 ounces, which was not enough to pay the bills. The Cathroy Larder, or Mirado, Mine delivered 10,231 ounces of low-grade gold but was only worked for six years spread out between 1941 and 1987. The only other producer on record in the camp was Gold Hill in Catherine Township, which parted with 660 ounces in the late twenties.

One shaky Boston Creek mine was guaranteed to fail when the directors began to consult a medium any time they wanted to sink a shaft. The Kennedy Boston was said to be producing gold but shut down when the payroll was hijacked. The area's biggest claim to fame was a frequent summer visitor in the thirties and forties, Albert Anastasia, who travelled in a bullet-proof car when he came to stay with mine owner Alfie Bargnesi and other relatives. The Mafia kingpin made no more visits after 1957 — he was gunned down by Crazy Joe Gallo in the barber shop of New York's Sheraton Plaza Hotel.

The bush between Gogama, Westree and Shining Tree just east of Highway 144, north of Sudbury, has seen exploration and work on scores of properties since 1911. Most of the activity has taken place in Macmurchy and Tyrell townships. Gold-bearing veins have been found throughout the area in Keewatin-type metavolcanics. Several prominent Canadian mining firms have been involved over the years in properties that had small headframes and mills but now remain only as expensive holes in the ground.

There is gold in the district but it is low-grade and erratically distributed. Statements in provincial reports and company accounts of the area have varied greatly — a sure sign of firms "gilding the lily" as they attempt to give their properties a promising sheen for investors. The Lake Caswell prospect, 8 kilometres west of Shining Tree, had a shaft sunk to 159 metres. In several incarnations since 1919 much drifting has been done on four levels. "Spectacular gold samples" were touted in 1926, but subsequent work has not rewarded the searchers. The nearby Bilmac prospect has had six different owners and names since first staked in 1911. There was a 130-metre shaft, much lateral development, and an 80-ton mill. In 1933 a 12-ton sample gave up all of 8.45 ounces of gold; no one has been able to coax out any more since.

So far there have only been two producers in this hard-luck camp. The Rhonda Mine property was discovered 6.4 kilometres northeast of Shining Tree in 1912 by two prospectors working for A. Ribble. Until 1939 the site was owned in succession by several mining companies. Each deepened the mine until finally the shaft reached 213 metres via a winze. Finally, at the outbreak of the Second World War, Rhonda Gold Mines installed a 150-ton mill and took out 27,727 ounces of 0.11-grade gold before closing in 1942. Periodically the property gets a going-over by optimists. The most recent efforts were by Triton Explorations in 1977.

The biggest producer in the camp and the one that holds the most promise is the Tyranite Mine, 22.5 kilometres northeast of Shining Tree. Prospector

L. Hedlund found the occurrence in 1932 while trenching claims. Over the next seven years it was optioned by five interests, one of which was the M.J. O'Brien firm. Tyranite Gold Mines obtained backing for a plant in 1938 and erected a 200-ton mill. Wartime material and labour shortages forced closure in 1942, but not before a handsome 31,352 ounces of 0.14-grade gold were produced from the 343-metre shaft. The mine never reopened after the war and the place stayed dormant for more than 40 years. Then, in 1986, flow-through financing enabled $4 million to be spent on shaft rehabilitation, a new headframe and a surface plant. The brand-new property worked intermittently and is currently closed. Additional funds are hard to find in the current investment climate. Owner Northfield Minerals needs $1 million to access near-surface gold. There is no doubt the mine will work again. New investor money forgets where old venture capital was lost.

Whereas Shining Tree became known as a broker's happy hunting ground due to its many dud properties, Matachewan, to the east, became the biggest producer in the small golden triangle. Provincial geologists saw gold there as early as 1900, but several years passed before prospectors made any interesting discoveries. The area took its name from the Matachewan River. It was not until 1916 when Jack Davidson discovered the yellow metal in an irregular mass of quartz and rusty weathered schist that prospectors began to walk the ground in earnest. A year later Sam Otisse made a find in reddish porphyry adjacent to Davidson's claims. Both properties languished during the First World War and the recession that followed.

Weldy Young promoted interest in Davidson's claims in 1924, but nothing significant happened in the area until 1930. Then Bert Ashley made a rich discovery in quartz veins among the greenstone in Bannockburn Township. The price of gold was rising and this justified development. Alex Mosher, fresh from his discoveries in Pickle Lake, played a key role in staking what became the Ashley Gold Mine. Production commenced in 1932 with a 125-ton mill. The mine only worked four years but paid out 50,123 ounces of 0.32-grade gold. The success of this venture influenced the development of the earlier discoveries in this new mining camp.

Young Davidson Mines made progress when Hollinger Consolidated Gold Mines of Timmins took over the operation in 1933 and erected a 500-ton mill. At first the ground was worked as an open pit, giving up 0.10-grade gold. But though the deposit was low-grade, the gold was present in close to 7 million tons. This, combined with the activity of its neighbour mine, kept the village of Matachewan prosperous for more than two decades. The Young Davidson Mine produced the best output of any of the mines in the triangle. Before the mine closed in 1956, all of 585,690 ounces had been shipped. By then a shaft and winzes had taken the underground activity down to the 324-metre level. Since that time Pamour and its successor Royal Oak Mines have leased the property and done much diamond drilling.

Sam Otisse's claims became Matachewan Consolidated Mines — the second-largest gold producer in the triangle. Once Ventures and Sudbury Basin Mines took over this property in 1933, the place settled down to steady production alongside the Young Davidson Mine. Although this mine had a slightly higher grade, at 0.11, the output was less — 378,101 — ounces and the mine closed in 1954. In recent years, mining rights were obtained by Pamour, which hoped the old producer could be worked profitably again once gold prices climbed. Later, Goldteck Mines secured recovery rights to the gold-rich tailings. The mine had been closed

The Stairs Mine at Matachewan had high-grade ore but was only worked from 1965 to 1966. – PA 145354

for 36 years when, on October 17, 1990, Otisse Lake overflowed into the tailings pond. Traces of lead, zinc and nickel in 170,000 cubic metres of mine slimes flowed into the Matachewan River, putting drinking water for Matachewan and Elk Lake at risk and threatening fish stocks. By the time the dam was repaired and other clean-up work was done, the costs came to about $1.5 million.

The province took action to recover a portion of the costs from the owners of the long-abandoned mine site and its current lessees. This action caused a furor in the mining industry. Goldteck paid out $40,000 as a goodwill gesture but the others fought the case. They argued that Ontario was applying 1990s regulations to an enterprise that had followed the existing rules when it closed 40 years before. This was the second time that a mine in Matachewan had been the subject of regulatory controversy. In the early seventies, political action had closed the Midlothian Asbestos Mine even before it came into production. Only one other gold property produced in Matachewan. The tiny Stairs Mine operated from 1965 to 1966 and delivered 3,573 ounces of 0.23-grade gold.

Recent years have seen a surge of optimism in the small golden triangle. Royal Oak announced it would plan for production at the Young Davidson property. The aggressive company had outlined more than a million ounces of low-grade gold left behind by former miners. A Native land caution was lifted early in 1995 and a staking rush took place. Eventually, more headframes will stand on the horizon in this area.

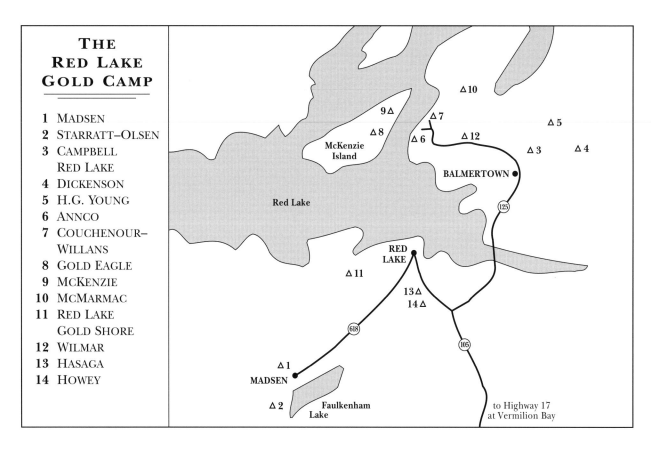

THE RED LAKE GOLD CAMP

1 MADSEN
2 STARRATT–OLSEN
3 CAMPBELL RED LAKE
4 DICKENSON
5 H.G. YOUNG
6 ANNCO
7 COUCHENOUR–WILLANS
8 GOLD EAGLE
9 MCKENZIE
10 MCMARMAC
11 RED LAKE GOLD SHORE
12 WILMAR
13 HASAGA
14 HOWEY

McKenzie Island

Red Lake

△10
9 △
△8
△7
△6
△12
△5
△3
△4

BALMERTOWN

125

RED LAKE

△11

13△
14△

618

105

△1

MADSEN

△2

Faulkenham Lake

to Highway 17 at Vermilion Bay

Red Lake was the first mining camp in Northern Ontario where aircraft were used exclusively. A Bellanca and a Canso are at anchor in this October 1946 view. – Dickenson Mines

THE RED LAKE RUSH

There's lots more gold.
All you've got to do is go up there and look at it.
"WHIRLWIND" JACK HAMMELL

THE THREE GREAT GOLD RUSHES in the first quarter of the twentieth century were all centred around lakes. Kirkland Lake was filled with mine tailings. Porcupine Lake still survives in the Timmins camp. Red Lake, 109 kilometres long, is not only the largest but is also the most unspoiled of the three. Situated 150 kilometres north of Dryden, it is still a peaceful beauty spot, with only three small communities fringing its shores. The bays and peninsulas of its deeply indented shoreline are a delight for visitors and residents alike. According to a Native legend, blood coloured the waters after a monster was slain there.

In 1872 a Geological Survey of Canada geologist travelling south of Red Lake was told of interesting rock formations in the area but he was unable to visit at the time. A colleague, Dr. D.B. Dowling, explored the big lake in 1893 and reported that he had found some interesting minerals. This prompted a British syndicate to send a crew to Red Lake four years later. The party took the 320-kilometre land and water route from Dinowic on the CPR line. The long trip was rewarded when they found surface gold in a decomposed vein near the shore and staked eight claims. R. J. Gilbert, the leader, decided they would return south and engage a surveyor to verify the accuracy of their work, since the area had not yet been mapped by Ontario. The last man into the canoe, Gilbert reached for his belt and loaded revolver, which were still lying on the rocky shoreline shelf. In a freak accident, the weapon slipped from its holster and discharged, instantly killing Gilbert. Despite the summer heat and the long trail, the party packed his body out and reported the discovery to the syndicate.

J.B. Tyrell was the surveyor engaged to confirm the claim location. He was the brother of famed Canadian explorer Joseph Tyrell, known in connection with Kirkland Lake. The surveyor wintered in the Red Lake area. His work crew sank an 8-metre shaft and took ore samples that assayed a splendid 0.6 grade. Unfortunately the principals decided that the prospect was too remote to be commercially viable and the venture was abandoned. Another British group explored the area in 1912, but the arduous overland trip to the big lake forced them to the same conclusion.

This was the first provincial building in Red Lake. Ernie Holland (first left), the mining recorder, is next to an O.P.P. officer just flown into the camp. At the far right is Johnny Jones, a prospector from the Porcupine. – OA 6805 S11808

Various prospectors continued to work the area, but it was not until 1922 that it was visited by a large number. A rumour of silver deposits near the big lake attracted about fifty men who crisscrossed the land around the lake on the lookout for a mineral that simply was not there. The majority soon moved on, but one group found gold on McKenzie Island, situated in the fork of the Y-shaped lake. Herbert Tyrell and Fred Carroll found what would later become two good mines. On the mainland, Carroll staked out claims that would one day become the Cochenour–Willans Mine. Tyrell's stake on the island was eventually the site of the McMarmac Mine. No one will ever know how many prospectors searched the big lake in the early twenties. Two who never made it were Chris O'Kelly (a First World War Victoria Cross winner) and Bill Murray. Both men drowned in autumn 1922. When a passing Native found Murray's dog, a search was made and their fate was discovered.

One persistent prospector was Findlay McCullum of Winnipeg. He never found a big mine but did influence the men who made the first big strike. Brothers Lorne and Ray Howey of Haileybury were interested when McCullum showed them the 1922 report of Department of Mines geologist E.L. Bruce. This report indicated several areas around the lake where greenstone with gold-bearing quartz had been located. There were four in the party that set out for Red Lake in the spring of 1925. Lorne Howey and his brother-in-law George McNeely were grub-staked by hometown investors. Ray Howey and W.F. Morgan were working for McIntyre Mines with the guarantee of an interest in any discovery. The group spent the summer with little success and finished up camped on the south shore of the lake at a place that would later be called Howey Bay.

The men were ready to leave when McNeely saw gold-veined quartz at the base of a tree felled by a lightning strike. Lorne Howey followed this discovery up by stripping moss in a line from the tree until he found a 6-metre-wide vein with visible gold throughout. At the same time, Ray Howey and Morgan came across a 4-metre shear zone with an extensive outcrop of mineralized greenstone. They later realized it was the same vein. Most accounts agree on the exchange between the two brothers. "Looks like we've got it," shouted Lorne. Ray shrugged. "Ain't that what we came for?" he asked. "Now come and look at what I've got." Since the finds were made at the same time, they drew a line separating the discovery, with Ray's claims to the west and Lorne's to the east. Eventually the Howey and Hasaga mines would develop from their work. After more exploration, the happy four returned to seek outside capital. News of the lucky strike soon began to circulate in mining circles.

The Howey brothers told their friend Dan Willans of Haileybury about the gold at Red Lake. Willans was a mystery to most of his fellow prospectors. The polished gentleman with an Oxford accent who never talked of his past had no difficulty persuading his partners Bill and Ed Cochenour to come with him to the new gold fields. They arrived in September 1925 and hired a guide to take them to Red Lake. They staked the short-lived Buffalo Red Lake property, north of the Howey claims, and secured what would become the most successful Cochenour–Willans Mine. Other prospectors they encountered were "Hard Rock" Bill Smith and C.H.J. Cunningham. Smith's claims were not viable but he made up for it later in the Little Long Lac camp. Cunningham, nicknamed "the Major," staked claims that eventually became part of the Dickenson Mine. He did not stay in the area, but instead he sold some other claims for $30,000 and went off to seek his fortune in Quebec.

The Howey brothers needed substantial financing and they turned to "Whirlwind" Jack Hammell, so named for his early prize-fighting days. The burly promoter

After his Porcupine success, Sandy McIntyre found nothing at Red Lake but a good time.
Hopkins was one of the original geologists in the area (1926). – OA 6805 S11805

67

did not hesitate to accept the Howey proposal. He went to Red Lake to see for himself and took Alec Gillies, Benny Hollinger's old partner, to verify the nature of the ground. While at Red Lake, the promoter staked some claims on the site of the present town of Red Lake. On arriving back in Haileybury, he optioned his claims to Dome Mines and secured backing to develop the new Howey Gold Mines. Hammell took half of the property and the original stakers split the other half.

Hammell wanted to get supplies to the property before freeze-up. The flying boats of the Ontario Air Service gave him an idea. He applied to the province to charter several HJ2L aircraft, the old First World War "Jenny." The request was initially turned down, but Hammell won his way by arguing that the fire season was over and the idle planes could be earning their keep. Soon the Howey supplies were being air-freighted from the provincial air base at Sioux Lookout. This was the first time that aircraft were used in a Canadian gold rush. Soon other firms were offering air service. Hudson became the main shipping point, with freight at a pricey dollar a pound. Pilots such as "Doc" Oaks, Tommy Thompson and Frank Davidson led the way and started Patricia Airways.

While some goldseekers went by air, the majority sought their Eldorado in the new gold fields the hard way. The Red Lake rush shared the excitement of California and the Klondike in that there were as many romantic dreamers as seasoned prospectors. Their time was short — the great influx of newcomers lasted only the twelve months after Christmas 1925. The story was front-page news across the continent. *The Boston Post* had the poetic banner "Mush on Goes the Cry," while the *Ottawa Journal* headlined "Magnet drawing Prospectors." Weeks of hype were capped when a crew from Fox Movietone shot aerial footage of the rush, and within days the first motion pictures of Red Lake could be viewed at countless cinemas.

The adventurers going overland wound up at Hudson on the CPR line. As Charlie Chaplin's *Gold Rush* began to entertain the public, the goldseekers were coming to grips with life at the railway whistle-stop. Food and supply costs were high. Dogs for packing outfits inland were exorbitantly priced whatever their pedigree. All food for men and dogs had to be carried in to Red Lake. With lard at $1 a pound, sugar, $35 a sack, and flour, bacon, beans and tea to buy, the newcomers were at least light in the pocket on their travels. Accounts of the total number of fortune hunters vary from 1,000 to 3,000, with perhaps a hundred horse teams working the route for heavy freighting. Depending on the season, the journey could take up to six days. Comfort could be gauged according to the quality of outfit and size of bankroll. The three rough camps that offered covered shelter at stages on the way did a roaring business.

A reporter from the *Winnipeg Tribune* flew over the south shores of the big lake on January 2, 1926. He saw hundreds of snow-banked tents, their owners practically hibernating waiting for spring break-up to reveal the land. He landed and found them in good spirits despite the harsh climate and poor living conditions. Within one month, 3,500 claims were staked in the area. By the end of 1925, mining recorder Bert Holland, newly arrived from Kenora to set up his office in a tent, had registered more than 10,000 claims. Neb Faulkenham packed the official and his equipment into the camp and then stayed to open a tent-frame store and restaurant. The Province sent up a lone constable, Lawrence Carr, to maintain the peace. Eventually Ontario became more involved, sharing with mining companies the construction cost of rail links between portages. One freighter was George Wardrop, who was later minister of mines from 1961 to 1967.

Wardrop, who later used his stories on the campaign trail, was well known for his tall tales. According to one story, a pulp camp Wardrop used to run had a large tomcat. The cat chummed with the blacksmith and enjoyed his warm shop. The cat had caught his paw in a trap, froze it badly and lost the limb. The kindly smith made his pal a wooden leg. One night, on hearing a racket, men ran outside seek the cause. They found the cat — holding a rabbit with his sound paw and clubbing it with the wooden leg.

Despite the competition of many prospectors, there was still gold to be found. Marius Madsen, a young Dane who had emigrated to Canada in 1925, staked claims south of Red Lake. The property would one day be a big mine bearing his name, but 12 years passed before any gold was poured. On the way out, Madsen met up with Joe McDonough, who would later help him bring his mine into production. The St. Paul brothers took ground to the west of the Howey property, and it later became the Red Lake Gold Shore Mines. By late fall 1926, the majority of goldseekers had moved on, leaving only a small band of optimists behind. High costs of operating in a remote area scuttled small outfits. Prospectors found it harder to get grubstakes. Many properties were teasers with only scattered pockets of gold not plentiful enough to justify capital investment.

All of the properties acquired in the gold rush days of the Red Lake camp took several years to make into mines. The Howey Mine had a large low-grade deposit consisting of a network of quartz veins in a sheared and fractured porphyry dike. The width of the deposit fluctuated wildly. Jack Hammell realized that more capital was needed and Dome Mines optioned a seventy-five percent interest in the property for half a million dollars. But after spending only $50,000, Dome dropped its option. Hammell calmly picked up Dome's Howey stock, transferred it to the mine at cost, and looked for another big backer. He still found time and his own capital to create NAME (Northern Aerial Mineral Exploration), which operated eight planes and paid wages for a hundred prospectors.

W.S. Cherry, a wealthy Canadian living in Rhode Island, was looking for an investment and bought into the Howey. Hammell raised $1.5 million by buying more shares himself and also selling some to mine operators Al Wende and Harry Oakes of Kirkland Lake. The shaft was sunk 300 metres before they reached profitable mill-feed. At the same time, the mine was building a mill and subsidizing electrical service. The Howey spent $200,000 to build a 72-kilometre transmission line to carry power from a new generating station at Ear Falls. The investment was gradually returned in preferred hydro rates. The 500-ton mill went into production, and by careful cost control, the first mine to operate in the camp became profitable. An increase in the price of gold widened the profit margin, and patient shareholders finally received dividends in 1934. When the Howey closed in 1941 due to a collapsed shaft-pillar, increasing costs and wartime restrictions, it had achieved a Canadian record for low-grade output. The final production figure was 421,592 ounces of 0.19-grade gold.

The Red Lake Gold Shore was staked in 1926 but did not venture underground until 1934. The orebody was not large but seemed to be consistent. In 1936 the new mill processed 115 tons per day while shaft sinking continued. The ore had been found in quartz blebs and stringers, and when the sinking-crew reached 213 metres, the ore simply ran out. From a winze, they dropped down a further 87 metres, but in the words of one resident, there was not enough ore to fill your pipe. As the Gold Shore closed, Hammell eyed other land near the Howey. He picked the ground up for $110,000 and purchased the Gold Shore mill and plant. The new company surfaced as Hasaga Gold Mines. The property processed ore for 14 years with a total 218,213 ounces of 0.14-grade gold. A small mine on nearby McKenzie Island gave up richer muck at a 0.22 grade. From 1937 to 1941 the Gold Eagle Mine gave up a modest 40,204 ounces. A much more successful operation on the big island, McKenzie Red Lake Gold Mines, rewarded investors for more than 20 years. The camp's second-largest producer, it extracted 651,156 ounces of 0.28-grade gold before the 1966 closure.

The seven McDonough brothers are probably the biggest mining clan in Canadian history. Pete and Jack staked part of the McKenzie Red Lake and also the Cochenour–Willans in 1927. Joe McDonough joined with Marius Madsen to make the most consistent and profitable of the mines that resulted from the first Red Lake gold rush. By 1934, Madsen had established the property in the Falkenham Lake area (11 kilometres south of Red Lake) but was having difficulty financing the project. Joe promoted it and raised the capital. In 1936 one of the original stakers, Austen McVeigh, found a rich shear zone north of the area under examination. A shaft was sunk and production began in 1938. With the addition of more property in 1941, the Madsen turned out to be richer than the Howey, and a community grew up around the mine. The shaft was deepened to 1,524 metres in 1954 and the mill was extended to process 1,500 tons a day. The Madsen was good to its shareholders, operating until 1976 with a total production of 2,416,609 ounces of 0.29-grade gold.

The second largest of the Red Lake mines that started in the thirties took many years to become a viable operation. The Cochenours and Dan Willans found plenty of gold showings on their claims east of McKenzie Island. But the place was a teaser. There were no large veins or dikes. The deposit was irregular, appearing to have no pattern in its complex and tiny veinlets. The partners took Jack Hammell's idea and syndicated the property to allow them to do surface work. Funds ran out, but they were fortunate enough to option the area to Ventures, the famous exploration company. The firm sampled the ground and did some drilling but could not solve the problem of the complex ore structure and dropped its option. Dan Willans went back to prospecting. The Cochenours finally interested Hollinger Consolidated in taking an option in 1935. The deal was likely the last one Noah Timmins made before his death. Hollinger Consolidated spent $100,000 sinking a shaft to the 83-metre level. Drifting provided good ore values but no consistent averages. Hollinger took its exit and the persistent partners were once more without backers.

W.P. Mackle, then manager of the McKenzie Red Lake Mine, encouraged the despondent owners and told them the occurrences of high-grade ore should make a mine. The Cochenour–Willans Mine was incorporated in 1936 and Mackle joined as resident engineer. Bill Cochenour was not much help for a while because his

The McKenzie Red Lake Gold Mine had its own townsite and miners did not have to go far to fish. – Author collection

partner Dan Willans had disappeared and he was away searching for his long-time friend. Meanwhile Mackle followed through on his hunch that ore on the property was in lenses, or podlike deposits. When financing was tough, he took his salary in shares to confirm his confidence. He cut a raise at the 45-metre level and found strong ore values. Five thousand tons of this ore was milled at the nearby Gold Eagle Mill, and the venture was rewarded with a return averaging between $17 and $23 a ton. Despite an earlier disappointing appraisal of the property by engineer John "Turn 'em Down" Reid (so called for his rigorous mine viability reports), the embattled principals now knew they had a mine. A 150-ton mill was in operation by September 1939 and now there was no shortage of investors. Despite the uncertainty of wartime operations, the mine performed profitably until February 1944 when lack of manpower and supplies forced a temporary closure.

While the mine was idle, the property of adjoining Kelson Red Lake Mines was acquired. The mine was on a sound footing and would produce 1,244,279 ounces of 0.54-grade gold before it closed in 1971. Dan Willans, the gentlemanly prospector, disappeared from his camp close to the Teddy Bear property northwest of Kirkland Lake. The public trustee took over his affairs and interest in the Red Lake mine and offered a reward both in Canada and the United Kingdom for information regarding Willans, but without success — Willans was never found. Haileybury friends speculated that he was ill and took his own life when he felt unable to withstand the rigours of bush life. Bill Cochenour always mourned his lost partner. He believed Willans would have been proud of their mine, which took 14 hard years to put together.

Gold was discovered in 1927 at Uchi Lake, 85 kilometres east of Red Lake. Jack Hammell used his energy and promotional expertise to build the mine there. It took eight years to establish the operation. Until the province built a road from Gold Pines to the mine site, Hammell used aircraft and heavy barges to ship in freight. By 1939 there was a surface plant and accommodation for single men, but when three more claims were added in 1942, the place boomed to 350 employees. A townsite was constructed with a bank, a school, a community hall and a curling rink. Good ore lasted only until 1943, but 114,467 ounces were recovered, making it well worth Hammell's while. After closure, much of the plant and its buildings were shipped elsewhere. The rest of the site remains, quietly decaying at Uchi Lake.

Marmac Red Lake Gold was made from an amalgamation of the Margaret and Richmac properties. It was a modest venture that operated from 1940 to 1948 and returned 45,246 ounces of 0.30-grade gold. Not far away, the Duncan Mine on Narrow Lake showed free gold at surface but none could be found underground and the place closed in 1930. The Bathurst and Bobjo mines never made money and the Red Lake Mammoth Gold Mine is just a memory. The manager of the Jackson–Manion became so despondent at his inability to raise funds to keep his charge going that he committed suicide.

H. Dewitt Smith formed the Newmount Mining Company in 1935 to tap a gold property north of Red Lake on Berens River. The property was so far north that it was easier to drive an access road from Lake Winnipeg, Manitoba, than to venture north from the established mining camp. When Ontario and Manitoba refused to subsidize a year-round road, Smith built one himself. By 1940 there was a townsite housing 600 people, of which 210 were mine employees. The mine was forced to build its own hydro plant as well, as neither province had power lines stretching that far north. Dewitt's mine lasted until the ore ran out in 1948. During its production years, 157,341 ounces of 0.28-grade gold were recovered. The plant was dismantled and the townsite left to the elements. The road is now impassable, and with present access by air only, the buildings are a well-preserved monument to a once-bustling community.

In 1946, twenty years after its gold rush, Red Lake had a road out to Highway 17 near Vermilion Bay. The new approach to the gold camp would soon be busy. George Campbell sparked renewed interest in the Red Lake camp. His brother Frank was in the party that discovered the Dome Mine in Porcupine, and its leader, Jack Wilson, married George's sister, Ida Maud. George did some prospecting and his brother Jack and cousin Colin staked the Red Lake Gold Shore property. George spent several years methodically exploring the area around Balmer Lake. Prospectors had difficulty in understanding the geology of the area because it was covered with overburden up to 2 metres in depth and there were few outcroppings.

George, Colin and their partner, A.K. McLeod, staked claims at Balmer Lake in 1944. George was the leader, sporting a rakish fedora even in the bush. They received some development funds from promoters Arthur White and Jack Brewis. The financiers eventually set up Campbell Red Lake Mines. Meanwhile the three prospectors found rich surface showings. There was no difficulty in selling shares.

Dome Mines became interested and took the company over with a fifty-seven percent stake. At the same time, White was dealing for the neighboring ground with mining engineer C. J. Dickenson and broker Irving Isbell. He financed Dickenson Red Lake Mines with the money he received from the Campbell enterprise. The Campbell began production in 1949 and produced $18 million in gold in just six years. Massive deposits of visible gold were common in the workings. The time was ripe for what has been called the second Red Lake gold rush. Labour and capital were freed from wartime restrictions and a host of companies became active in the camp.

George Campbell soon made up for 20 years of hard times and hard work. Ignoring begging letters that followed after the press broke news of his success, he bought cars, boats and airplanes, the latter being used to further prospecting ventures. Campbell played the part of a mining magnate to the hilt. He drank heavily and ignored pills prescribed for a heart condition. Four years of fast living took their toll and, in 1949, at the age of forty-eight, he died of a heart attack. His wife, Gene, continued to live at their Hell's Acres cabin (so called because George said the land was hell to clear) until her death in 1989. She was a feisty, tough-talking pioneer. Famed photographer Karsh came to capture her determined air on film some years before she died. The mine George Campbell named succeeded beyond his wildest dreams. Over the years it has given an average 0.6 grade. The low-cost operation has been Placer Dome's biggest money-spinner. In 1993 the annual production was a record 300,472 ounces, and in that year, the Campbell poured its 8-millionth ounce of gold since the mine started. With reserves estimated for at least 13 more years, the Campbell stands with the Hollinger, Lake Shore and Kerr Addison as one of the great mines of Canada.

The other currently operating mine, the Dickenson Red Lake Gold Mine, was first staked in 1926 by C.H.J. Cunningham-Dunlop (known in the trade as "the Major").

Mines Minister George Wardrop and Dickenson Red Lake president Arthur White, general manager F.A. Fell and mine manager J. Gillies at the mine's 2,000th gold bar pour.

– Mines Library

Souvenirs of Hell's Acre, the Campbell cabin. Shown is a portrait of Gene Campbell by Karsh.

– Placer Dome

He had to let it go for lack of capital. G. J. Dickenson bought a half-interest in 1944 after it was re-staked by Gordon Shearn. The place took off when Arthur White and Jack Brewis took a third of the property for $25,000. The growth of the nearby Cochenour–Willans Mine made investment capital easier to find. As the second mine in Balmour Township, the new mine had a faster start-up than the Campbell, since there was more exposed bedrock and much surface trenching had already been done in the thirties. Brewis and White sold their interest in the Campbell to concentrate on the then-more-promising Dickenson Mine.

The Dickenson poured its first gold in December 1948. The mill had been purchased from the Gold Eagle Mine on McKenzie Island. The place is now known as the Arthur White Mine. All the precious metal won at the mine has been a result of careful engineering and planning. In contrast, the Campbell has had an embarrassment of riches. The ore at Dickenson is structurally complex, so considerable drilling and development has always been necessary to keep track of locations for mining. For several years the mine has produced around 75,000 ounces annually at a 0.39 grade, reaching its 3-millionth ounce in 1993. A new bio-leach system at the mine should increase reserves by conditioning flotation concentrates before cyanidation. Arthur White chuckled when asked if he regretted taking the Dickenson over the Campbell in the early days of both properties. The mine, after all, brought him a fortune and the 80-year-old was inducted into the Canadian Mining Hall of Fame in 1991. New owner Goldcorp changed the official name to Red Lake Division. The long-established mine promises to keep paying dividends for many years to come.

Jack Hammell had one more property in Red Lake. The ground near the Madsen Mine had been first staked in 1926. The stakers were David Olsen, R.W. Starratt and W. Cooke. The resulting Starratt Olsen Mine was worked by Hasaga Mines from 1948 until closure in 1956, after having mined a modest 163,990 ounces of then-marginal 0.18-grade gold (a fraction of that enjoyed by the neighbouring Madsen Mine). Following the Starratt Olsen, the H.G. Young Mine came into being in 1960. The ground was originally staked by George Campbell and actually had its shaft on Campbell property. In its three-year life the mine produced 54,244 ounces of 0.19-grade gold.

The Red Lake camp is very active today. The Madsen Mine still has reserves of three-quarters of a million tons and the property is being rehabilitated for operation. The old Cochenour–Willans and several other former mines are under active assessment. Current gold prices are the only bar to development of known ore. As Terrence Podolsky of Wilanour Resources has pointed out, "The business of calculating reserves is a little like beauty; it's in the eyes of the beholder."

The Campbell Red Lake Mine has recently improved hoisting to 1,200 tons a day and the mill output runs to 1,500 tons daily. There is a new column-flotation circuit, which has improved recovery, reduced power consumption, and provides consistent concentrate for the pressure oxidation plant. The big mine has a huge recreation centre complete with a curling rink, bowling alley and an Olympic-size swimming pool. No wonder the Campbell Band sings, "I'm a Campbell miner, I know how to rock. I'm a Campbell miner, pushing that Placer Dome stock." Placer Dome knows it has a rich cash cow in the Campbell. At a grade of 0.7, it is the richest gold mine in Ontario, returning a staggering 323,168 ounces in 1994 alone.

A meeting of routes underground at the Dickenson Mine. – Dickenson Mines

The Kirkland Lake camp was built around seven mines in close proximity. At Red Lake the producing mines spread out over a wide area and several small communities developed. The town of Red Lake has recently been joined by Golden (an amalgamation of McKenzie Island, Balmourtown and Cochenour). Communications and transportation are good, but it still remains a frontier area, looking to Winnipeg as the big city, a five-hour drive away. Mining talk always excites residents. It has, after all, been a billion-dollar gold-producing area and the geology still holds much potential. With 110 known gold occurrences in the area, there are bound to be more gold mines in the historic Red Lake camp.

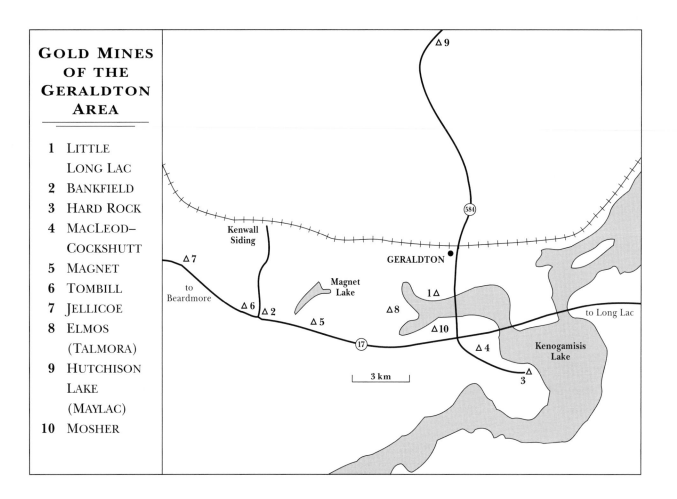

GOLD MINES OF THE GERALDTON AREA

1 LITTLE LONG LAC
2 BANKFIELD
3 HARD ROCK
4 MACLEOD–COCKSHUTT
5 MAGNET
6 TOMBILL
7 JELLICOE
8 ELMOS (TALMORA)
9 HUTCHISON LAKE (MAYLAC)
10 MOSHER

Kenwall Siding

to Beardmore

GERALDTON

Magnet Lake

to Long Lac

Kenogamisis Lake

3 km

T.H. Rea, George Rayner, Tony Oklend, Joe Errington, J. Waite, Boul and two unknowns at Little Long Lac in the early thirties. – Geraldton Public Library

LITTLE LONG LAC

We're destined to find the big one today. Let's get going!

BILL "HARD ROCK" SMITH SAID THIS DAILY
UNTIL IT WAS FINALLY TRUE IN 1931.

LITTLE LONG LAC sits astride Highway 11 between Geraldton and Long Lac. What is now known as the Beardmore–Geraldton mining area stands on Keewatin greenstones and Temiskaming sediments. There are greywacke and iron formations and intrusive rocks of porphyry and quartz diorite. Bedrock is buried beneath swamp, marshes and glacial till, with few natural outcrops. For many years iron was the only mineral of interest in the area noted by geologists, but had they looked more carefully they would have found gold in the greenstone.

In 1917, T.L. Taunton, a field man with the Geological Survey of Canada, found gold around Little Long Lac. He noted its lustrous gleam in quartz fragments found along the shore but wrongly concluded that it was transported by glacial action because he saw no glint in the quartz veins. He might have met Tony Oklend while crisscrossing the waters of the big lake. An immigrant from Lithuania, Oklend had come to work as a navvy on the railway. He saved his pay and wound up as a contractor, grading the track near Geraldton. The newcomer liked the area and began prospecting, financing trips by trapping on the side. During the First World War he hit a small pocket of high-grade in a boulder near the main narrows of the lake and chiselled chunks out of it to pay for supplies. He was discreet, for while stories of his small find spread, no one found the spot. Oklend would be associated with the precious metal in a much bigger way later.

Favourable reports by government geologists brought prospectors to the area between Long Lac and Nipigon in the twenties, but no significant discoveries were made. It fell to Bill "Hard Rock" Smith to make the first big find in the district. Smith was a veteran prospector and had claims next to the Howey in Red Lake, but they were not on rich ground. He was an enthusiastic prospector in what was often a hard-luck profession. In later years, famed mining man Murray Watts recalled working in the bush with him. Each day the older man roused his young partner with the feeling that it was it was the day he would strike it big. That special day did not take place when the two were together. Smith found his gold while prospecting with Stan Watson south of the west narrows of Little Long Lac in the summer of 1931. The partners staked eighteen claims around three veins but only twelve were subsequently recorded.

Smith was now in a bind. He wanted to advise T.H. Rea, a principal in the Hard Rock Prospecting Syndicate, which was financing the venture, as to the extent of their discovery but did not want to tip off other prospectors who habitually took their ease in the telegraph office. He solved the problem by sending the exciting news to Toronto in a letter. The communication took only two days. Rea replied promptly by the same means, telling him to spend some more time and money channelling the surface showing and then to bring the samples to the city. Smith and Watson's eventual reward was ten percent of the syndicate shares. Smith did send one telegram. Assured of his own success, he wanted to help out prospector friends Fred MacLeod and Arthur Cockshutt. His wire caught up with them at Amos, Quebec, although perhaps not as promptly as they would have liked. When the pair asked an operator if there was a telegram for them, they were told there was nothing new. On a hunch they pulled out a stack of flimsies from a pigeon-hole and found Smith's message buried in the pile. They jumped the next train west, but other prospectors were already ahead of them.

Veteran staker Tom Johnson was to become the most prolific and successful prospector in the area. In the fall of 1931 he was teamed with Robert Wells. The two men visited the Hard Rock discovery and then worked their way from Little Long Lac down Magnet Creek to Magnet Lake. Johnson noticed quartz with gold in a shear zone on an outcrop in the middle of the lake. Part of the claims they took that day would become the Bankfield Gold Mine. Early in 1932 Johnson found another zone at the same location and staked more claims to the west; in time these became the Tombill Mine. Johnson was impressed with Tony Oklend's experience in the area and persuaded him to team up in June 1932. Oklend showed his new partner where he had found the gold that had financed prospecting trips. Nothing there impressed Johnson and they toured Little Long Lac from the west arm to the main narrows. On July 5, Johnson led the way to investigate a square face of rock shelving on the shoreline. He noticed the presence of bismuthinite, a dark grey mineral that is often a host to gold. As they paddled along the shore to check a similar location, Johnson spotted gold in quartz in the clear water. He jumped out of the canoe into the knee-deep water. The partners soon found several specimens holding rich visible gold. The showings were so good that the excited pair hurriedly staked twelve claims before other prospectors arrived. Oklend had worked 20 years in the bush and knew that at last he had his mine. As for Tom Johnson, the ground they had taken was the most important of several mines he found.

MacLeod and Cockshutt left the train at Langmuir, a CNR flag stop north of the lake. As they paddled south, they were followed by Jock MacGregor, another prospector. They found Smith's discovery claim and were prepared to stake when Smith arrived and suggested that they take ground to the west of his claims. This was done and they laid out fifteen claims without interference from MacGregor. Both newcomers had been prospecting across Canada, but this time they had a payoff for all their years of hard work. Fred MacLeod was quite a storyteller. Once he yarned about it being so cold in Labrador that the mountain goats, attempting to jump from peak to peak, froze stiff in midair. One listening greenhorn argued that this was impossible, for it defied the law of gravity. Fred smiled and said it was so cold that gravity froze as well.

Developer Joe Errington is flanked by prospectors Art Cockshutt and Fred MacLeod, who hold the first gold bars poured at the MacLeod–Cockshutt Mine. – Geraldton Public Library

By the summer of 1934 a gold rush had opened up the area from Long Lac to Nipigon in a belt 100 kilometres long and 40 kilometres wide. The Sturgeon River gold district to the west eventually became known as Beardmore. For the purposes of this book, this area is considered one camp. Because it was the Depression era financing arrangements for mines were dropped if preliminary development results were not conclusive. So it was that properties discovered in 1932 could take from two to six years to make a mine (in one case, 20 years). Today the mine sites are clustered near Highway 11, but in the thirties there was no road. At that time, access came by the railway to the north from stops such as Langmuir, Hard Rock, Jellicoe and Beardmore.

At first the settlements were so spread out that it seemed little had changed since the first gold strikes. A village grew up at Hard Rock in 1934. It became larger than the "stopping place" envisioned by Maud Gascon when she opened an eatery and bunkhouse there. Similar places grew up at Longlac, Bankfield and Geraldton. All of these spots went through a roller-coaster ride of development and slump as the mines struggled to warrant production. Industry observers knew the settlements were in for the long haul when residents finally decided to paint their houses. A major forest fire in 1936 ravaged the district. Some buildings were burned at the three principal mines and only a concerted effort saved the properties, but Geraldton escaped the flames. Life had returned to normal when Geraldton passed a by-law, signifying that the frontier town had entered a respectable era: cab drivers were not to give rides to women of ill-fame or persons of bad character.

A new headframe under construction at Hard Rock Mine (1936). – PA 14864

The Leitch Mine near Beardmore was one of the richest gold mines in Canada. It was staked by Karl Springer. – Geraldton Public Library

The Northern Empire Mine near Beardmore was called a "prospector's dream" and gave one third of an ounce to the ton (February 1934). – Author collection

The first mine in the camp to actually start up came from ground staked by Tom Powers and Phil Silams near Beardmore in 1925. Their telegram to geologist Percy Hopkins did not hide their excitement: "Have found a prospector's dream. Will hold till you come up." Hopkins was suitably impressed by a large vein carrying much visible gold. The Newmount Mining Corporation took over the property and started the Northern Empire Mine. Its main operation was from 1934 to 1941 but there were four other periods of activity between 1949 and 1988. Total gold production was 149,493, at one third of an ounce to the ton.

The Little Long Lac Mine opened in 1934. Geologist Percy Hopkins persuaded Joe Errington of the Sudbury Diamond Drilling Company to take over the project. Stakers Johnson and Oklend received a total of $50,000 and a ten percent interest in the mine. Errington became the main promoter associated with the camp. He brought in Thayer Lindsay of Ventures Corporation to help bring the property to production. Drilling revealed a huge ore-shoot plunging deep beneath the lake. Initial water troubles were solved by sealing seams with cement. The multi-veined ground was rich, and the average grade over the life of the mine was 0.34. Ore was accessed by shaft and underground winze, and the main shaft was sunk 1,205 metres by 1947. Geraldton was home to many of the miners. By 1939, when the highway came through, the town even had a golf course.

The war slowed production at all area mines. One of Little Long Lac's contributions to the war effort was the discovery of scheelite, a tungsten ore. The strategic metal was prized for its high tensile strength. The mine kept producing gold until December 1953 when ore reserves were exhausted. It produced 605,449 ounces of gold, then worth $22 million, at prices less than a tenth of current values.

In 1934, mining attention switched to the Beardmore area when J.M. Wood and W.T. Brown found the property that became the basis of the Sturgeon River Gold Mine. Well-known Cobalt-based Coniagas Mines held the major interest in the mine, and it produced 73,438 ounces of 0.50-grade ore from 1936 to 1942. The other mine from the same period, which can still be seen on Highway 580 out of Beardmore, was the Leitch Gold Mine, a bigger mine than its neighbour. Brothers James and Russell Cryderman found the property. The Leitch was incorporated by Karl Springer and gave the prospector a start as a developer in various camps. The Leitch was one of the most consistently high-grade plants in the country, averaging an almost unheard of 0.92 grade from 1936 to 1968. Some 861,982 ounces were obtained in that period. In three other operations concluded in 1988, a further 6,985 ounces of a lower grade were recovered. Rich gold tailings remain but the surface plant is gone and mine houses were trucked away to Beardmore and Jellicoe.

The ever-busy prospector Tom Johnson returned to the Magnet Lake area with his brother Bill. Percy Hopkins got involved, and with Newmount backing, Tombill Mines was formed in 1935. Johnson's original find with Robert Wells would make a mine first. As Bankfield Gold Mines, the claims were proved by Joe Errington's drilling firm. Values found at Bankfield were associated with pyrites, common in other camps but rare to the Long Lac area. A big party celebrated the first gold pour in June 1937. A small townsite was built and its hockey team, the Bankfield Millionaires, were strong district contenders. But the Bankfield success was short-lived. Despite extensive exploration, the mine closed in 1942 after producing only 66,416 ounces. It was worked again from 1944 to 1947. Johnson's other discovery, the

The Bankfield Mine in 1941 a year before the ore run out. – Author collection

Tombill Mine, ran from 1938 to 1942 and produced 3,000 more ounces than the Bankfield at a higher 0.36 grade. The nearby Jellicoe Mine was a disappointment, for it gave up only 2,000 ounces from 1939 to 1941. But to the east of the Bankfield, there was a much more successful venture. The Magnet Mine began in 1938, using the Tombill mill until its own facility was built. It worked until 1943 and then again from 1946 to 1952, using claims bought from the now-closed Bankfield Mine. In all, 152,089 ounces of rich 0.42-grade gold were recovered, making it the best producer in the area.

The Hard Rock property, which caused so much excitement when it was first staked, took six years to make a mine. Smith's backer, T.H. Rea, chose Joe Errington as vice president and optioned the ground to Homestake Mining Corporation, which did much assessment work but later dropped the option. Finally Hard Rock Gold Mines raised its own funds. After initial failure, it hit gold ore in porphyry, iron and quartz stringers. Spectacular visible gold soon convinced investors to pick up the shares. The mine began operating in January 1938, and tonnage rose each year until it peaked in 1942. But as with other mines, the war years meant difficulty in keeping miners. The Hard Rock closed in 1951 after having given up 269,081 ounces at an average grade of 0.18, one of the lowest in the camp. When the enterprise closed, Mosher Longlac came along and purchased the plant and equipment.

The biggest producer at Long Lac, the MacLeod–Cockshutt, was one of the last to get started. Ventures, Dome, and later Fred Connell all worked the ground between 1932 and 1935 but quit when veins seemed erratic and ore values low. This left the original stakers in control. With shares sinking to a rock-bottom nickel apiece, they used the remaining treasury to drill. They found better grades near Hard Rock's Porphyry Hill. By now, Joe Errington had exercised an option and as more money came in shares soared to $4. The mine finally began delivering mill feed in April 1938. As for Joe Errington, he died four years later — before his last great venture, the giant Steep Rock iron project, began producing. In 1940 the MacLeod–Cockshutt bought two claims from the Mosher interests and settled

The remains of the once great MacLeod–Cockshutt Mine, June 1992. – Author collection

down to solid production until 1970. In all, the mine handsomely repaid share-holders, giving up 1,516,980 ounces at a 0.14 grade (although considerable output in the early years was very rich). In 1958 this veteran mine's fortunes were linked with those of the Mosher Mine when Little Long Lac Gold Mines acquired both properties.

Murdoch and Alex Mosher staked claims that tied into the MacLeod–Cockshutt to the west in 1934, but it took two reorganizations, 27 years, and three connections with the adjacent producer before the place became the Mosher Mine. In 1950 the Moshers acquired the old Hard Rock ground. It was only when Little Long Lac took over that the cost of so many years of exploration was finally recovered. In 1968, the concern was amalgamated with the MacLeod–Cockshutt Mine, which was then working on a recovery clean-up. During the Mosher period and the amalgamation salvage time, it produced over half a million ounces of gold. The Little Long Lac camp covered a large area. Many mines such as the Theresa and the Tashota–Nipigon operated in the district but few such small outfits made any money.

The Beardmore–Geraldton mining area has plagued prospectors due to heavy glacial overburden which obscures native rock. Diamond drilling has taken away the mystery. Founder Resources, Hemlo Gold and Placer Dome are firms now active in the area. Both the Magnet Mine and the Pan Empire mill are being main-tained for further work. One of the most interesting centres of gold activity is east of Longlac where the Hard Rock Extension Company is working (the firm has no connection with the original mine of that name). They have opened up four gold occurrences and figure that, since the camp produced 3,000,000 ounces between 1930 and 1968, the best place to explore is near former gold producers. American Barrick is following that strategy by carrying out extensive drilling on the former MacLeod, Mosher and Hard Rock mines to prove up remaining ore in those once-active producers. As the price of gold rises, new mines will start up again between Beardmore and Longlac.

Al Brazeau diamond drilling in the early days of the Central Pacific Gold rush. – MNDM

The Albany River Gold Mine never made money. – MNDM

Leslie Frost (first left), later Ontario premier, and Roland Michener (second left), later governor general, and other visitors listen to a shift boss discuss the merits of the Pickle Crow Mine. – Mines Library

NORTH OF
SIOUX LOOKOUT

*There is much more to this life
than a mad scramble for dollars.*

JACK HAMMELL, MINEMAKER

THERE WAS A SMALL GOLD RUSH north of Ignace around the turn of the century. Most activity centred around 70-kilometre-long Sturgeon Lake. The only moderately successful property was the St. Anthony Mine. It operated at the north end of the lake in 1900, but production was mainly from 1934 to 1942, providing 28,266 ounces from several quartz veins. The Golden Whale (later Sakoose Mine), near Dyment, was the centre of a group of small mines that in 1899 came to be called the New Klondyke. Unfortunately none of the mines there were profitable. Only the Sakoose produced in later years (1944 to 1947), with a modest total output of 3,328 ounces.

The main mining action in the area was to be further north. The Red Lake gold rush sparked other exploration in the Patricia District. NAME brought hitherto isolated areas within the reach of goldseekers. In 1928 two prospectors working for the NAME syndicate found gold along the Crow River. John MacFarlane and H.H. Howell staked the first property, and within a year 225 claims had been taken. Out of this activity came two good gold producers. Unfortunately the 1929 financial crash put NAME out of business. It had been one of Jack Hammell's best projects and located many good properties in the North.

Transportation problems slowed development of the mines north of Sioux Lookout. The promising ground was 160 kilometres north of the CNR line, but the only practical entry was via a roundabout 273-kilometre water route. Eventually the mining interests formed the Lake St. Joseph Transportation Company. Supplies and equipment came via Hudson, just west of Sioux Lookout. Tugs towed scows east over Lac Seul to a 5-kilometre link of marine line called the Root River Railway. Each barge was floated onto a partially submerged flat car and then moved along by a small gas locomotive before it was refloated. At the east end of Lake St. Joseph, trucks completed the journey with a 40-kilometre haul to the mines. The trip took ten days and freight charges dramatically increased start-up costs.

The original advertisement for Jack Hammell's Pickle Crow Gold Mines featured sketches of a dog-team, a tractor train and aircraft, all completing the link to a headframe. The market was assured of "a consistent high-grade gold-ore deposit." Some wag on the Toronto Stock Exchange dubbed the Pickle Crow "a drunken bird." Hammell was enthusiastic but the promoter had great difficulty in obtaining financing. Unable to attract what he referred to as O.P.M.(Other People's Money), Hammell put up $115,000 of his own to float the venture. Those who took Pickle Crow shares were not disappointed. The ore was high-grade and the mine set a record in paying dividends just 11 months after the 1935 opening.

Alex and Murdoch Mosher staked the Central Patricia property in 1927. Although the brothers were involved in many successful mines, they were no strangers to tough times and hardship. Alex thought that flying was only for "big shots." Instead, the two prospectors used a dog-team. One time in the Patricia District, the only food they had was cornmeal, which they had to share with the the dogs. "We ate all the same fare," recalled Alex, "but the dogs' food was cooked in a separate pot and we added salt to our own meals. It was grand to arrive at a camp where they had some real fat bannock." Fred Connell took over promotion of the ground they had staked. Although it was incorporated in 1929, there was no significant activity until 1933. Like Pickle Crow, the Central Patricia had power problems until Ontario Hydro put up a plant 41 kilometres to the south on the Albany River. Electricity reached the mines in 1935. The first Central Patricia manager, Allan Anderson, had his own adventures moving equipment until the two mines joined to set up their own transportation system. Once, a tractor train heavily laden with mill components broke through the early ice and all the sleds it was hauling sank to the bottom. Anderson had no experience in diving but he borrowed an air hose and suit and went below to examine the sunken equipment. The next summer it was salvaged and in due course the mill was erected on waiting foundations, none the worse for a winter-long dip.

The Pickle Crow Mine had veins that did not pinch out at depth as some critics had predicted. By 1937 the mill was processing 400 tons of ore a day with a rich 0.45-grade average. The company town built by the Pickle Crow Mine had more than a hundred homes as well as a hospital, a store, a school and a church. Over at the Central Patricia Mine, 8 kilometres to the south, there was a community of similar size. Both mines had problems keeping labour during the war years, but in 1945 refugees from overseas were pleased to accept jobs in the Pickle Lake area. The Central Pat lasted until 1951 and produced 621,806 ounces of 0.36-grade gold. The mine and townsite were sold and most buildings were moved to other locations.

The days of lengthy and costly transportation were over in 1956 when Ontario completed Highway 599 from Dryden to Pickle Lake. The community of Pickle Lake grew while the original townsites in the area declined. Jack Hammell, a former boxer turned mining promoter, had brought several mines into production. He died in 1958 at the age of eighty-two. On the day of his death he finished a bottle of champagne. His two nurses received $50,000 each, for he said they had kept him alive by watering his whisky. The mine he had financed finally closed in 1961. Low gold prices and increased costs brought an end to the Pickle Crow Mine, which had repaid investors with 1,446,214 ounces of gold. Ten years later the property remained derelict and the Ministry of Natural Resources burned what was left of the buildings.

The Crowshire Patricia Mine (October 1946) was a small gold mine near Sioux Lookout.
– Author collection

Miners wait for the cage at the 670-metre station of the Pickle Crow Mine after their shift (September 1941). – Mines Library

The "suite" at the Pickle Crow Hotel in the early forties. After the mine closed and there appeared to be no more chance of development, the Ministry of Natural Resources burned the community down. – Mines Library

Night drilling at the Musselwhite property. A huge gold deposit has been found in an area where there are no roads or hydro. – Placer Dome

Drilling in the stope at Dona Lake (1989). – Placer Dome

There was a lull in development but gold continued to be found around Pickle Crow and is still the preferred target of prospectors in the area. Placer Dome located a handy deposit close to the community and spent $43 million in the mid-eighties to bring its Dona Lake Mine into production just 12 kilometres to the southwest. The small but high-grade gold deposit was found in folded sulphate in replaced iron formation. The projected output of 40,000 ounces a year through the 500-ton-per-day mill was close to target and the grade improved to 0.24. The company employed Native residents in the area, and at the 1988 opening, guests each received the gift of a bag of wild rice. Once the mine was opened, the transition was made from tracked to trackless mining and this helped to control costs. Placer Dome turned over mining to Ross Findley Ltd., however, slim reserves forced mining of the crown pillar and a shutdown in 1994. The mill was dismantled and set up to work at the Madsen property in Red Lake.

Another major company found gold near Pickle Crow around the same time as the Placer Dome work paid off. Bond Gold, now part of LAC Minerals, found the precious metal 70 kilometres west of Pickle Crow in 1985. The Muskegsagagon Lake deposit of the Golden Patricia Mine centres on a narrow, steeply dipping quartz vein in the greenstone. This is unusual in that it is the only vein system noted in that area and it extends for 7.8 kilometres. The initial grade of 0.50 was high enough that the mine was brought into production less than three years after the first drill hole was put down. The Golden Patricia is a fly-in operation. Employees rotate on a two-weeks-in, two-weeks-out schedule and make the trip from Dryden. An ice road serves in winter months for heavy transport. The shrinkage stoping operation is accessed by two ramps, and an ore-only shaft to the 325-metre level was put down in 1991. The 350-ton-per-day mill has returned 48,000 ounces of rich 0.57-grade gold annually in its two years of production. New owner American Barrick is exploring its long-vein length to locate more mill feed and keep the mine open.

A huge gold deposit located 120 kilometres from Pickle Crow has been under examination since 1981. Placer Dome and TVX Gold have outlined the Musselwhite property at Opapimiskan Lake. The proposed mine would require an outlay of $100 million to reach the production stage. The partners face the same problem their predecessors did in the northwest in the thirties — the site is remote, there is no nearby infrastructure, and power lines are nonexistent. Diamond drilling in 1993–94 outlined a sizable orebody. The drilling was done from a barge platform on Opapimiskan Lake. A production decision should be made by late 1995.

Former producers Pickle Crow and Central Patricia still have reserves but are likely too small to be mined at a profit. Exploration continues throughout the district and several locations are worthy of examination. There are many gold occurrences in the Sioux Lookout district and new gold mines will be working in this area before the end of the century.

The Williams Mine on a clear winter night. – International Corona

The Winston Lake Mine is a base-metals operation that produces some gold. – R. Sim

THE RICHES OF HEMLO

*The best place to look for gold is
where gold is known to be.*

DON MCKINNON, PROSPECTOR

THE MINING DISTRICT from Schreiber to Manitouwadge never produced enough gold to encourage investors until recent times. Between 1897 and 1941, five gold mines milled a total of 5,176 ounces. The Empress Mine was low-grade, but the Gold Range, Harkness–Hays and Schreiber–Pyramid had good results over low output. The best producer, the North Shore Mine, ran from 1923 to 1941 and gave up 2,441 ounces at a rich 0.64 grade. Today, the Winston Lake Mine, a copper-zinc producer just north of Schreiber, delivers around 6,000 ounces of gold annually as a by-product. More gold is produced by this base-metals mine annually than the total output of all the early area gold mines.

The Hemlo district offered glimpses of the gold beneath it for more than a century before the great discoveries were made. A Native prospector saw gold showings near Heron Bay in 1869 and a little ore was shipped. Local CPR station agent J. LeCour dug some test pits after noticing promising mineralization in railway rock cuts but his claims lapsed when no further work was done. It was not until 1944, when Peter Moses (a Heron Bay Native) discovered several gold traces, that outside prospectors became interested in the area north of Lake Superior. One such prospector was an American radiologist, Dr. J. Williams, who dabbled in prospecting on his trips north. He staked eleven claims near the gold area Moses had found. He also joined with Moses and others in 1947 to stake what became the Lake Superior Mining Corporation property. Geologist Trevor Page worked closely with Williams in a search of the ground, but the Lake Superior group ran out of enthusiasm and gave up its interest. Teck Hughes Mine had the place for ten years but outlined too little ore to make a mine. Williams died and the claims remained in his estate. The area was staked and dropped by four outfits. From 1973 to 1976, Ardel Explorations had the property and outlined double what Teck Hughes had found, but it was still not enough to make a mine. A firm named Copper Lake had it next, and geophysical work showed very promising gold values, but problems within the company caused it to drop the claims. Thus it was in 1979 that what some would later call the richest chunk of mining land in the Western hemisphere was vacant when Don McKinnon came along.

Don McKinnon was a Northerner — a former forestry worker who first made a successful venture into prospecting in the Texas Gulf discoveries of the early sixties. In the seventies, family tragedy left him with time on his hands. He spent some of it with Walter Baker, an old-timer who had worked in the Hemlo area many years before and seen promise in the rich deposits. McKinnon's forte was always the amount of time he spent in research before entering the field. He traced Page's work and all other data relating to Hemlo. In 1979 he went in to stake as soon as the ground came open.

Don McKinnon and John Larche were both in the Hemlo bush just after Christmas 1979. They had known each other for years and had even done some work together. This time, Larche was doing some contract staking and McKinnon was following his usual research-motivated star. Big, friendly John Larche had spent most of his life in the mining game. At 15 years of age he had convinced the people at Preston East Dome he was three years older and won a job diamond drilling underground. As for McKinnon, his high-school principal had predicted he would end up digging ditches. McKinnon chuckles and affirms the crystal ball gazing was dead right, "It's just that I find gold in them!" Toward the close of 1979, McKinnon and his son David staked twelve claims at Hemlo. Larche discovered that claims McKinnon thought were taken were in reality open and staked seven more. The men decided to pool their new property and share equally in any profitable result.

David Bell, a Timmins-based geologist, deemed that their claims were valuable, but the two prospectors found it tough to convince Bay Street financiers of the potential of bush ground near Manitouwadge. Finally the paperwork on the property was taken to Vancouver, where promoter Murray Pezim looked the material over. While this was going on, Larche and McKinnon picked up some grubstake money from investors in Timmins and Toronto to take first 156 and later 12,000 claims. The excitement of mine financing can rival that of on-the-ground work. Murray Pezim supported another Vancouver trader, Nell Dragovan. Dragovan had a shell company, Corona Resources, which was fresh out of assets. Pezim might have been seen by many as a hustler but with his engaging manner was the star money-raiser on the Vancouver Stock Exchange. He did his part by raising $1.2 million for Corona so that exploration work could be done at Hemlo. Eventually he bought the major interest in Corona through one of his own companies.

David Bell became Corona's consulting geologist. After some initial diamond drilling he decided that since the gold was not in veins and seemed to be widespread, it might be a primary deposit. He advised Nell Dragovan to acquire as many claims in the area as possible. She turned to Don McKinnon to track down Dr. Williams's widow in order to make an offer on the claims. In the meantime, LAC Minerals was also interested in the Williams claims. LAC had gathered extensive information about the adjoining ground and expressed interest in a possible joint venture with Corona.

Don McKinnon dutifully found Mrs. Williams and made the offer, but a senior official with LAC convinced her to take its offer instead, even though it turned out to be half of what Corona would have given. At the same time, Bell was directing many costly drill holes. This sent Pezim scurrying for extra financing. It was a cliffhanger all the way, but hole number 76 struck values of 0.21-grade gold over 3.2 metres. By hole 120, a huge orebody had been outlined. Pezim, now on

The huge grinding mills in the Williams Mine concentrator. – Teck Corp.

Corona's board of directors, was delighted. Only a few months after *The Northern Miner* had scoffed that the find was more than likely one of Pezim's promotion myths, he was suing LAC for breach of trust in the acquisition of the Williams ground. Pezim contended that Corona had first call on the claims and that LAC had violated a trust. As for Larche and McKinnon, their years of hard work had paid off. By December 1981 each was worth about $5 million and climbing.

Murray Pezim brought the Teck Corporation in as a partner in order to gain working capital. Frank Lang and Richard Hughes obtained claims from Don McKinnon and sold them to Noranda. So there were now three companies at Hemlo. Noranda called its mine the Golden Giant. As ever, a gold rush started once the best ground had been taken. Claims were staked for 80 kilometres around. Hopeful investors jumped at shares of companies with "Hemlo" in the title. None amounted to anything.

By the end of 1984, LAC had outlined $5 billion in gold at the Williams property. For Murray Pezim it was a bitter time. The promoter had overextended himself. His brokers called in their margin accounts and he had to sell his controlling interest in Corona. He was ousted from the board of the company that, through his support, had been the first prominent player in the Hemlo camp. The following year he would at least gain satisfaction from observing the course of the ownership battle between LAC and Corona. A five-month-long trial ended in March 1989 and saw LAC lose the Williams Mine. Corona and Teck took the plant and the profits made since the start-up. LAC received $154 million to cover its cost in building and operating the mine. This was $50 million less than the actual expenditure, but the judge ruled that had the Bell and Williams orebodies been worked as one mine, only one mill would have been required. Finally, after all appeals had been heard, Corona and Teck had the biggest gold mine in Canada.

A roadside sign reading Yellow Brick Road points to the Hemlo gold camp. The skyline, with its three mines, signifies the largest working gold area in Canada. In 1991, the combined output of the three mines made up half the total Ontario gold production and twenty-three percent of the Canadian output. This comes to about a million and a quarter ounces of gold.

About five years passed from the time the properties were staked until they began to produce gold. The Williams Mine began to operate in December 1985. The largest of the Hemlo three, it is also one of the biggest gold producers in Canada. Williams's sheetlike 2.45-metre-wide orebody contains fine-grain gold and molybdenite with barite and sericite. The big mine uses both blast-hole and open-stope mining, and backfills with a delayed cement and rock mixture. No gold mine in the country comes near its 6,000 tons milled per day. Joint owners Teck and Corona worked open-pit recovery first, and funds from this effort helped finance underground development. In 1994 the mill delivered 445,320 ounces with an average grade of 0.22. This is a much lower grade than the other Hemlo mines but reserves are much higher. The mine has 611 employees and a life-expectancy of at least 15 years. As for International Corona, the company merged with Homestake Mining and the resulting firm is the biggest gold miner on the continent.

The Golden Giant Mine, owned by Noranda and Hemlo Gold, is made of original interests in Goliath, Golden Scepter and Noranda Mines. This property mines in continuous retreat sequence, from the bottom up and out in pyramid fashion. The ore flow is fully automated, from ore passes to mainstream haulage, crusher, loading pockets, shaft-hoisting, and finally, to mill coarse-storage bins. All mine systems are monitored by computer. Cables and outlets reach all key points underground. Stationary, hoisting and pump systems are checked at night by the maintenance coordinator from his own home using a computer with a modem. In this way he can pinpoint and diagnose problems and even direct on-site staff to take action. The Giant has a grade of around 0.36 with a moderate reserve. The mine still put out 446,858 ounces in 1994. At current production, the 314 employees should have at least 15 years of work ahead. Just beyond the Golden Giant main gate is a smooth-rock outcrop. At the crest a sign proclaims "Mount McKinnon, elevation 1.37 metres." The rock is quartz sericite schist and is the host rock for the gold. Before mine construction such features were common but this is the last one left. Don McKinnon prevailed upon the owners to save the little pile. It is one of the few reminders of the area as it was before gold was taken from the ground.

There is a quarter-claim fraction between the Giant and David Bell mines that is accessed through the Golden Giant's 1,145-metre shaft. Net profits are divided between the two owners. The smallest of the three Hemlo properties, the David Bell Mine, owned by Teck and Corona, is well suited to mechanized mining. The preferred extraction method in this mine is blast-hole mining. The 1,600-ton-per-day mill finds the ore a challenge to process due to a high antimony and sulphide content. There were 200 workers at the mine in 1994 when it produced 204,251 ounces at a 0.44 grade. The Bell may be small but it has the lowest production costs of any gold mine in Canada and is one of the lowest-cost operators in the world.

The Hemlo gold mines had given up more than 6 million ounces of gold by the close of 1992. Exploration in the area goes on. Currently the Schreiber area looks promising in the search for gold.

PROSPECTS AT HARKER HOLLOWAY

Below ground only the miner can shake hands with ore.

ARNOLD HOFFMAN, *FREE GOLD*

NORTH AND SOUTH of the 60-kilometre stretch of Highway 101 that runs east from Matheson to the Quebec border near Duparquet is an area that has lacked neither prospectors nor mines since 1909. A great number of elegant share certificates languish in bottom drawers across the continent — issued by companies once active in the mining game but now out of business. There were scores of small mines such as the White–Guyatt in Munro Township, which gave up 10 ounces in 1911, and the Aljo in Beatty Township, which recovered 40 ounces in 1940. Mines such as the Painkiller Lake, Potter, Doal, Cryderman and East Remo put money into the ground but never took anything of value out. Eighty years passed before American Barrick built the first substantial mine, the Harker Holloway.

In the thirties, King Midas Gold held two veteran's lots in Munro Township east of Matheson. A good general rule of thumb for prospective investors is to avoid junior mining companies with fanciful names. The King Midas, for example, contained no gold. But just a short distance away, in Munro, there was a high-grade gold mine with ore so rich that it is said to have had the highest grade of any mine in Ontario. In the spring of 1914, a prospector named Walsh found a spectacular gold showing in the first concession of Munro. Unhappily for Walsh, when the claim was surveyed, his showing was found to be just 4.57 metres inside the adjoining claim. The Dominion Reduction Company of Cobalt bought all the ground and named it the Croesus Mine. The gold came from a quartz vein in Keewatin diabase and pillow lava and the property was worked from 1914 to 1918. In 1915 *The Northern Miner* reported that "one gold nugget was egg shaped, two inches long and one and a quarter across," and "there was so much gold in the rocks that breaking them was difficult." In 1916, it reported that "the Croesus high-grade ore surpasses anything yet found on the continent both for persistence and fabulous riches."

In the initial four years of production the shaft reached 121 metres, and 515 metres of drifting took place on six levels. Rich ore was even taken during shaft sinking, which assayed 5,945 ounces to the ton. Surface gold near the shaft was of such high grade that the company covered it with a steel plate and padlocked the

The Croesus Mine was one of the richest mines in Canada, but most of the ore was in the shaft (1916). – Ontario Archives

cover in case the treasure walked during the night. The surface property was destroyed in the Matheson fire of 1916, and several miners were among the estimated 243 dead. Although the plant was rebuilt and a small mill was added, the mine closed in 1918. Since that time there have been at least four periods of operation and several name changes. Much of the gold taken after 1918 was recovered from the dump and in a general clean-up. Official records up until 1936 show an output of 14,859 ounces with a record 2.79 ounces to the ton. Production has taken place since 1936, but the ore was shipped directly to the Mint and no record has survived to the present. The gold at the Croesus was free, coarse and easily visible. One observer likened the deposit to plums in pudding.

Between 1917 and 1925 no less than sixteen companies were engaged in exploration in the Harker Holloway area. Harker Gold Mines had a shaft sunk to 305 metres. Five other firms in the area also went underground. The most prominent in the field was the Mining Corporation of Canada, which did considerable trenching and sampling in 1924 but with little success. The present American Barrick property in Holloway Township is situated on ground discovered by prospector P.A. McDermott in 1922. A company bearing his name did some trenching and diamond drilling and even sank a small shaft on the gold-bearing alteration zone currently being mined. Low grades discouraged further work and the operation shut down. Just prior to the outbreak of the Second World War, the Consolidated Mining and Smelting Company worked the McDermott claims, but with best values found at no greater than a 0.16 grade, concluded that the ore was not commercially viable.

Kirkland Lake's Sylvanite Mining Company had an equally fruitless experience with the same ground in the late forties. It was not until almost four decades later that the prospect became part of the exploration holdings of Camflo Mines. Exploration manager Dit Holt and his assistant Dick Harding went over all the old files they could find relating to work done since the twenties in the Holloway area. They concluded that the property merited more attention. Gilles Tousignant led the ground search, and a good surface zone was located with values averaging a 0.12 grade, but this promising news was put on hold by the 1982 recession.

Ruins of the Croesus mill (1962). – Mines Library   *Ruins of the Croesus headframe (1962).* – Mines Library

Two years later, Barrick Resources, the forerunner of American Barrick, gained control of Camflo and with it the services of Dit Holt. He made a deal with Bob Kasner of Lenora Resources and other claim holders around the McDermott property and secured enough ground to support a low-grade mining operation. Then came more than a year of geological detective work and surface preparation. Among those involved was geologist Al Workman. He found a significant fault that cut across the ore zone at a shallow angle, partially controlling the distribution of ore. He named it the McKenna Fault (after his father-in-law). The orebody was further delineated with seventy-six drill holes, totalling 18,288 metres. It was then plotted by computer.

American Barrick made the decision to go ahead with mine development and within two years the $78 million Holt–McDermott Mine was ready to produce gold. Sixty-four years had passed since the nucleus of the property was first staked. Holt and McDermott were honoured in the name, though McDermott would never know it. He disappeared in the Lightning River area in the late twenties while on his way to work claims and was never heard from again.

The Holt–McDermott Mine is about a 45-minute drive from Kirkland Lake, on Highway 672 past Esker Lake Provincial Park, 6 kilometres east of its junction with Highway 101. A sign at the mine gate proudly announces its record as district mine rescue champions. The blue steel siding of the mine stands out as the only dash of colour in the surrounding bush. Since the mine's opening in 1988, the operative word at this plant has been "lean." Financial restraint is evident in the small work force and the economy of operation. Manager John Haflidson emphasizes that the mine has stayed viable in a low-grade deposit situation through careful planning and cost control. In its early stages, the average mill feed was a scant 0.15 grade.

An aerial view of the Holt–McDermott Mine.   – American Barrick

The Holt–McDermott Mine is within the Abitibi Greenstone belt, the host rock to mines from Chibougamau in the east to Hemlo in the west. The property's McKenna Fault is possibly an offshoot of the Destor–Porcupine Fault, which hosts the gold-bearing strata of the great mines of the Timmins camp. Ore deposits sit in basaltic volcanic rocks along the fault. Chief geologist Murray McGill has said this mine was "made, not found." The orebody is long and narrow, like a plate standing on a 68-degree-sloping edge. The main production zones are spaced along it like bubbles. The McDermott zone was mined first, then the Worvest, and later the Mattawasaga. The Mattawasaga had given up production from two surface pits in its early days. Since 0.20-grade ore has finally been located, operating costs have declined. The hoist can raise 1,500 tons of muck a day from the newly deepened shaft, and the refinery has a target of 100,000 ounces for 1996. The ore gets to the mill economically through innovative rock-extraction methods. Contract drillers with Boart Canada cut inverse drop-raises in long-hole open stopes. They can drive a raise 2 metres square by 15 metres in a long slice up from the bottom level. Such a big chunk of rock is removed through extremely accurate parallel drilling, careful blasting and the skill of an experienced raise crew.

Mill superintendent Lloyd Buckingham oversees a computer-monitored plant with an eat-off-the-floor atmosphere. The ultra-clean mill can extract as little as a tenth of an ounce of gold from a ton of rock and still recover more than ninety-four percent of its precious content. Broken rock is ground in the primary mill and further pulverized in the ball mill. The greyish pulp moves to the thickener and then on to the carbon-in-leach circuit. This process is used to prevent the loss of gold due to occasional deposits of graphite in the waste. In six stages the gold ore, free carbon particles and cyanide particles are mixed in a slurry. Using temperature, pressure, cyanide, and sodium hydroxide, retained carbon is stripped of gold. The process goes on 24 hours a day in a building operated and maintained by no more than three people at a time.

In the refinery room the whole purpose of the mine comes into focus. General mill foreman Bill Lupton generally works here alone. The gold-bearing solution is pumped from the mill circuit into a big metal box called the electro-twinning cell. The solution comes into contact with an anode and a cathode. The result is a brown sludge that collects on a section of stainless-steel mesh. Five of these sections, containing high-grade gold, are removed and then dried in an oven. Weighing determines how much flux is required. The operator, well protected with an apron, long gauntlets, safety glasses and a visored helmet, fires up the Duraline electro-induction furnace. There is no time lost while the furnace heats up, as the slag pot has to be reamed out and coated with a mixture of oil and grease. The moulds go on a trolley, and when the ring of fire in the molten interior appears right to the experienced eye, the furnace is tilted to run off the slag before pouring the gold.

A vacuum tube is inserted in the molten mass to take a 10-gram sample. The glass evaporates as the gold fills the space. The slender wire of gold is enough for the assayers. The furnace receives about 10 kilograms of gold flake and a similar quantity of flux — normally borax, sodium nitrate and silica. Another tilt of the furnace and a golden arc pours down into the heavy mould. The slag goes back into the furnace and the process is repeated while the first bar is allowed to cool, dumped from its mould and washed. As gold is a semiconductor, cooling is quite fast. Lupton remarks wryly that the yellow metal would be first-rate for kitchen pots and pans if only the price were right. The room is warm because the furnace throws out a heat of 1,079°C.

Each bar is cleaned with a wire brush and an air-driven needle hammer. The mine name and the bar number are stamped into the gold surface. Within half an hour of the arc of molten gold pouring from the furnace, the bar can be handled. The heft of 77 pounds of gold, concentrated in a volume not much greater than that of a building brick, requires a two-handed grip. These dore bars contain about eighty-seven percent gold and ten percent silver. A private refinery will separate the minerals and remove any impurities.

Of the nearly 1.2 million ounces parent company American Barrick Resources produces for the world gold market annually, approximately 60,000 ounces come from the Holt–McDermott Mine. A program of gold hedging, using a mix of gold loans, forward sales, options and spot-deferred contracts, has resulted in consistently high prices for its product even in a weak gold market and has given the mine financial stability and investor confidence. The potential of this camp was known for 70 years before a mine was finally brought into production. Barrick's Holt–McDermott Mine was a low-grade mine with long-term potential.

The presence of an operating gold mine always spurs local exploration. There are several companies with property in the two townships that give this camp its name but one prospect, 3 kilometres from the current producer, originally saw work done 70 years before. The pioneer firm was Teddy Bear Mines. As the Holt–McDermott was starting underground in 1988, Hemlo Gold and Freewest Resources decided on a joint venture in what is known as the upper section of the Lightning River zone. The forgotten Teddy Bear claims were now valuable and it

A mechanic at work underground in the Holt–McDermott Mine. – American Barrick

Blast hole drilling the footwall, second bench, Buffonta pit at the Harker Holloway camp. – Perrex

took a proxy fight between rival shareholder groups and agreement among property owners before exploration could take place.

The gold in the Lightning River zone is in fine-grain pyrite, which is an Archean lode-gold deposit formed by high-temperature hydrothermal systems. The top of the deposit is 300 metres below surface and is known as a "blind" discovery because there are no surface showings and all the overburden had to be drilled to find gold. The orebody was marked out after $7.5 million of diamond drilling. The payoff was an orebody containing 5.8 million tons of 0.27-grade gold. Then, from 1992 to 1993, another $12 million was spent on a temporary headframe, a 441-metre exploration shaft, and underground bulk sampling.

The orebody outlined and the grade of that ore guarantee that another mine will be under way in the Harker Holloway gold camp by March 1996. Planning for the venture, now controlled by Hemlo Gold, estimates a capital cost price tag of $58.7 million for a plant capable of hoisting 1,654 tons a day for ten years. There is no need for mill construction, with Holt–McDermott facilities so close. The plant will be highly mechanized to provide superior safety for underground workers.

Ten companies are currently involved in exploration in the area along Highway 101. Glimmer Resources has a property 8 kilometres west of Matheson that has at least 410,798 ounces of gold and will likely be the next mine in this now-established camp. Other firms with promising claims are Gwen Resources, Kingswood Explorations and Central Crude. Eventually these and other companies with viable deposits will find backers and make new mines. The Harker Holloway area has taken 70 years to prove itself but at last has a number of promising orebodies to confirm its reputation as a major Ontario gold area.

GOLD TODAY

*The Golden Age comes to men
when they have forgotten gold.*

G.K. CHESTERTON

ART BUCHWALD ONCE SURVEYED the steady demand for gold and suggested that the United States should end its love affair with the precious metal and turn to a junked-car standard. This would ease monetary woes and clean up the landscape. Old wrecks would be crushed to shoe-box size by the Federal Reserve Bank while gold was dumped in the nearest river. Since Americans junk cars faster than any other nation, he reasoned, their reserves would be the world's largest. Buchwald's novel approach to fiscal reform ignored one basic fact — the value of gold goes beyond the price dictated by the world market. Gold would be attractive even if it cost nothing. As soon as the gold was dumped in the river, hordes of people would be waiting to retrieve and carry it away.

Gold has declined in price for years and yet the world demand for it continues unabated. Much current output goes off the market and is hoarded in private hands. Gold is more widely owned than ever before. From 1934 to 1968, while the metal retained the same market value, the earnings of workers soared. Gold jewellery is now within the purchasing range of most North Americans. Men are beginning to wear more gold jewellery. The demand for the lustrous yellow metal reflects to the wealth of a nation.

The most common uses for gold remain in jewellery and coinage. The Mexican Fifty Peso, the Austrian Corona and the South African Krugerrand have all been surpassed by the Canadian Maple Leaf as the largest-selling bullion coin in the world. Such coins are portable, legal tender and take up little room in storage of large sums.

People still carry gold around in their teeth. The metal is chemically inert and durable. Britain's National Health service cannot afford gold in dental work, but in Sweden and Germany it is still popular. Some physicians use intramuscular injections of gold in solution to treat severe arthritis, and it is commonly used in many Eastern countries as a medical prescription component.

One growing use of gold is in electronics. The metal improves the conductivity of electrical connectors and protects microcircuits in transistor manufacture. A few years ago, annual world consumption of gold for electrical contacts was estimated at over 100 tons. Gold and its alloys have several features useful to the industry,

Liquid gold pouring into a mould in the Macassa Mine. – LAC

including thermal conductivity, ensuring rapid dissipation of heat, and resistance to tarnish and corrosion. Because it reflects radiation, gold plating was used to cover the tether cord for the first American to walk in space. For the same reason, gold foil is used in television cameras used in space. In commercial airliners, gold is used in electrical circuitry, and as heat reflectors on engines. Jet windows incorporate gold a millionth of an ounce thick to cut the glare and heat of the sun by reflecting its infra-red rays and to electrically de-ice and de-mist the glass. On the ground, building windows incorporate a similar gold film to fend off solar radiation and ease air-conditioning demands.

Prospectors have always found gold underground and in streams, but it can now be recovered in many other places. A tenth of Noranda's gold feed comes from scrap-metal recycling. A top mine such as Campbell Red Lake has gold grading 0.75 ounce to the ton, but from selected scrap the smelter may extract a whopping 2 to 5 ounces from the same weight.

Despite a constant demand for gold, the outlook for Canadian production in the nineties is not rosy. Prices are poor, many low-grade mines have closed, and exploration has dropped by half since 1989. There are fewer than twenty operating

Gold bars ready for the refinery.   – Placer Dome

gold mines in Ontario and far fewer advanced-development projects than in past years. Several gold firms have viable properties but treasuries too small to handle development. The federal and provincial governments are cutting back on support for the industry in the face of increasing demands on scarce tax dollars. People in the industry blame government for overregulation and taxation, which scares off risk capital. Small companies that have backing to commence operations are deterred by the price of bonds they must post for reclamation costs in case of eventual mine closure.

Grass-roots campaigns such as "Save Our North" work for the development and protection of resource industries. Persuasive statistics are offered to back their argument that the industry needs help. Of every 25,000 claims, only 500 will be worth drilling and probably only one mine will be developed. They stress that reclaimed mining land can be redeveloped as park areas. Ontario's mines provide thousands of jobs and pump billions into the economy and yet do not take up as much space as that used by the Macdonald–Cartier Freeway from Windsor to the Quebec border.

There may be hard times in mining, but gold can still attract the spotlight. Miners take comfort in the fact that prices have slumped since the mid-eighties and are now beginning to turn around. In the meantime, gold is cheap and demand is strong. Most important, mining people are optimists. Right now prospectors are out in the bush searching for good showings and mining companies are evaluating prospects. Much of the $300 million spent annually on mineral exploration and development in Ontario is devoted to the lustrous yellow metal.

Texas Gulf stakers Don McKinnon, Ned Bragnola, John Larche and Fred Rousseau in July 1964.
– D. McKinnon collection

Viola MacMillan became the most prominent female prospector and developer in Canada. The mineral gallery at Ottawa's Museum of Nature, which opened in 1992, was named after her (March 1951). – Mines Library

Hemlo discoverer John Larche panned for gold near Atikokan but without success. – J. Larche Collection

PROSPECTORS AND PROMOTERS

*Gold is a very devilish thing
...it changes your character entirely.*

B. TRAVEN, *THE TREASURE OF THE SIERRA MADRE*

PROSPECTORS HAVE LAID THE FOUNDATION of the mining industry but only in recent times have they received the credit for the discoveries they made. Many prospectors seem to have a feel for where minerals might be found. The rock hammer is one of the few prospecting tools that has survived to the present. The handy gadget can scrape off moss and chip rock samples. Modern practitioners of the art usually start with a hunch and then turn to government maps done by aerial survey. These can pinpoint areas of electromagnetic activity, variations in magnetic fields and geochemical differences. Of four recent new mines, only one was found by prospecting alone. The others came to light via expensive drilling, airborne magnetometer survey and ground geochemistry. Miner's licences now cost $25, and claims are no longer limited to 16 hectares. They can be taken in blocks as big as 256 hectares. Claims must still be laid out on an east-west, north-south grid with four corner posts.

When the mining company takes over depends on various factors. The prospector could be a company employee or a contract staker. If a prospector is on his own, trenching, sampling and drilling can become an expensive proposition. Early prospectors sold their claims as they found buyers. Their modern counterparts may hold on longer but in the end will either sell the property or work out some kind of a deal.

The prospector still looks for shearing, alteration and gossans (rusty zones), which are visible markers. Gossans, quartz, and stringers may hold gold, but samples still need to be analysed in a laboratory. Analysis of elements present in stream and lake sediments, soils, humus and plant material can indicate the presence of gold in geochemical exploration. Homework always follows field trips. Results of past exploration are studied, and the stratigraphy is examined to pick out intrusive rocks that may have provided heat sources to move gold along from volcanic sources. Lithology locates the host and source rocks. A study of structural geology helps pinpoint regional structures where mineral deposits may be found.

The prospector is the first link in the mining chain. He or she (for there have always been women in the field) is first on the ground in the search for precious or base metals. In the early days prospectors only staked mineral prospects they could see. If the gold was not visible, they had neither the education nor the backing to stake ground on the expectation that it might be mineral-rich.

Arnold Hoffman shares accounts of two old-time prospectors, one of whom, Jack Davidson, worked alone, ranging across Canada. He would travel without a tent, slinging a hammock between two trees and just ignoring the flies and weather. Sometimes he made a concession to his need for creature comforts and waited out bad weather in a cave. Claims Jack Davidson long since abandoned have become mines. The Young Davidson Mine at Matachewan honoured his perseverance, but Jack never did become rich. Sam Otisse staked the area adjacent to the Young Davidson and his discovery became the Matachewan Consolidated Mine. Like many a prospector before him, Sam decided to enjoy life before the money evaporated. He bought a car, filled the back seat with canned goods (a staple of all prospectors) and headed west. Eventually supplies ran low and he recalled the words of his now-friendly bank manager — that he should contact the bank at once if he had a problem. Sam sent the man a wire: "Have run out of canned goods. Stop. Ship 500 lbs. Immediately. Stop. Signed Sam."

Reuben D'Aigle, in the Porcupine, saw gold but did not feel it was of sufficient quantity or grade to be worth claiming. Sandy McIntyre found surface showings and then unloaded them quickly. His partner Hans Butner saved his money but never made much from his hard work. Today's prospector is more knowledgeable than those who went before him. After all, he has the history of a century of gold exploration in the province to draw on. Two prospectors who have spent many years in the bush and have become well known in the industry are John Larche and Don McKinnon. They serve both as an inspiration and example to all who search for mineral wealth in Ontario.

John Larche left school in 1943 when he was 15 years old. The war was on and it seemed to make more sense for him to be out working. He had various jobs before turning up at the hiring office of the Preston East Dome Mine in South Porcupine. No one paid much attention to his birthdate or his lack of experience, because miners were in scarce supply. John worked as an underground diamond driller and over the next five years was employed at the Pamour and the Hollinger. Then he gave up mining for surface exploration. He was available for blasting, line cutting, claim staking and any work that came along.

While Larche worked for others he also did some staking for himself. As he explained to his wife when they married, this sort of life would see hard times but there was always work of some kind for an experienced bush man. With gold pegged at $35 an ounce in the fifties and sixties, he was glad to get work of any kind, for there was no strong incentive for mining exploration at the time. He was partners with Don McKinnon on occasion and made some money selling claims in the Texas Gulf staking rush in the early sixties. Dealmaking is part of the prospector's trade. With that success came a personal commitment to work full-time for himself. Larche knew that one day he would make a good minerals find because he was totally committed to the search. He was an active member of the Prospectors and Developers Association and never passed up an opportunity to learn more of his trade. He continued to comb the bush and promote the claims he held. Selling claims would put food on the table and finance another round of prospecting.

Larche and McKinnon staked the Hemlo field together. There was no visible gold on the site. What made the land interesting was that so many competent people had explored it before and much money had been spent. Earlier drilling had been done with small-diameter drills but they had missed the main orebody. When Larche staked his Hemlo claims, gold was surging beyond $500 an ounce and exploration money was easier to come by. McKinnon's claims covered an area where earlier work reported high geochemical samples, so it figured that the adjacent land held promise. As usual, a handshake between the two prospectors was sufficient to pool their claims and split any proceeds down the middle. A year passed before money flowed to the two men who had found the richest gold field in Canada. Both were used to making deals, but in this case development only came from aggressive promotion. McKinnon and Larche receive a net return from the smelter operation on the claims they staked. This means they hold an interest in the actual output of gold for the life of the mines. The proceeds have made them wealthy men.

John Larche no longer has to scramble for funds. He can afford his own aircraft instead of sharing a second-hand machine with partners. There is a house in Florida and a bigger home in Timmins with a swimming pool. The big, sturdy, smooth-faced man with a calm, direct gaze easily recalls his prospecting days and events to 1991. But there is a blank for August of that year. Larche and prospector-friend Harris Hanson were en route in Hanson's Beaver aircraft to examine some claims in Eskay Creek, British Columbia. They encountered bad weather west of La Ronge, Saskatchewan. As Larche was trying to climb above the clouds, the plane slammed into a mountainside. Hanson was killed and Larche suffered multiple fractures and other injuries. After plastic surgery and other operations, he has made a remarkable recovery with few scars, but his memory of the event is gone.

John Larche still has investments in the mining game. When he receives a clean bill of health he wants to go prospecting again. He is anxious to use his experience to locate more prospects. The veteran's advice to newcomers is simple: "Find out all you can about an area and look up all the records before walking the ground. Take along a good share of patience and stay fit. Times are tough but not impossible. Even if there is only one chance in several thousand of taking a rich property, any prospector could be the one to find an orebody."

Murray Pezim describes Don McKinnon as enthusiastic and honest. He could add curious, scholarly and driven. McKinnon left school early to work for a logging company. He worked as a timber walker, surveying stands for cutting. He did not turn to prospecting until the early sixties. Money from staking Viola MacMillan's ground in the Windfall property at Texas Gulf gave him his start. Since that time he has staked and sold claims across Canada. The self-taught goldseeker took his share of local geology courses but used his own special brand of research based on years of bush experience to find gold. He has built up a large library of Northern mining literature and there are few mining recorder's offices where he has not spent hours poring over both archives and current files. He still thirsts for

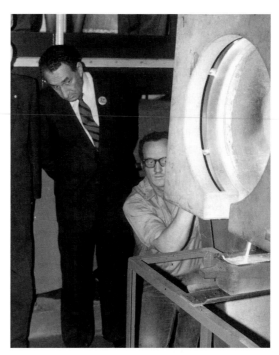

Don McKinnon and John Larche receive their first royalty cheques from Teck president Norman Keevil on May 29, 1985. – J. Larche Collection

Murray Pezim watches the first gold pour at David Bell Mine (May 29, 1985). – J. Larche Collection

knowledge, and his office near the Timmins airport is awash with papers. McKinnon has worked hard all his life — even the wealth accruing from Hemlo has not slowed him down.

McKinnon spent long hours articulately presenting evidence in the court battle that deprived LAC Minerals of the mine at Hemlo. Those hours are counted as time lost when he could have been out in the bush. He is now likely the most prolific claim-staker in Ontario. Including his antique cars, one of his few passions outside of mining, he owns more than seventy vehicles, most of which are heavy construction equipment for use in exploration work. Unlike Larche, who likes to pilot his own aircraft, McKinnon keeps a nine-seater beauty with his own pilot ready to take him to the next opportunity. His geologist is usually a member of the party.

Don McKinnon has gained prominence not only for his prospecting success but for his campaign to mobilize Northerners to see that decisions affecting the North are made in the North. He deplores what he calls mine bashing and legislated stumbling blocks to Northern development. Meanwhile there are few blocks to the prospector's own progress. In March 1991 his prospecting firm made a large zinc discovery in Hurdman Township near Smooth Rock Falls. After years of searching he has found his Eldorado but continues to use his experience and knowledge to benefit the area where he spent most of his life. McKinnon spends little time in his office. Most of the time the goldseeker is out on the trail of his dreams.

Prospectors with claims to sell usually meet up with promoters. Mining promoters find risk capital to finance new properties. Unfortunately Canadian mining has always been littered with promoters who spent more time fleecing the public than doing anything else. One of the more recent practitioners of the art, working out of North Bay, convinced investors that he had a high-grade copper mine when in fact no drilling had been done and the site consisted of a couple of holes in the ground. Such people make it difficult for those with genuine mineral projects to interest investors in parting with their money.

One prominent promoter who has done his share of creating wealth in Canada is Murray Pezim. Mark Twain's words are framed in his office: "October. This is one of the particularly dangerous months to speculate in stocks. The others are July, January, September, April, February, November, May, March, June, December and August." Unless a prospector can interest a major mining company in his property, the more likely route for its sale or development is through a promoter. The Vancouver Stock Exchange is the risk-taking capital of Canada, and Murray Pezim is its most well known stock mover. Pezim says a good promoter must have absolute faith in what he is doing, a good layman's knowledge of his product, and credibility with brokers in order to raise capital. He feels risk capital is more important to a developing country like Canada than investment capital because there is always risk in mining speculation. International Corona was just a shell company until it was promoted and used as the vehicle to develop Hemlo.

Nell Dragovan, a company director associated with the early development of the Hemlo gold camp, observes that no one invests in junior stocks with the grocery money. Yet many do enter the junior risk market, and if they lose their shirt, they blame promoters like Murray Pezim. The promoter's office at Prime Equities on West Hastings Street in Vancouver has a fine view of the harbour, but those who work there face inward to ever-ringing telephones and stock news feeding in on three monitors and an outsize television set. On one wall are testimonials to Pezim's work for charity. He has raised a million dollars for police and firefighters, charities, and a note from former prime minister Mulroney affirms that the promoter is "as good as gold."

Murray Pezim works at a long, curving desk. He scans current investment data and reads the mail and papers while speaking practically non-stop on the telephone. Calls frequently end with, "It's kosher, I tell you. It's going to go." In a lull between calls, Pezim recalls *The Northern Miner* citation in 1990 as Mining Man of the Year, for development of the giant Eskay Creek gold project in northern British Columbia. He admits that resource development has a huge price tag and, he would rather share or sell interests in good projects to major companies. In response to a comment about press criticism of promotion methods, he shrugs and says his creed is total honesty with the public. Investors will take a risk if they know the facts. Murray Pezim offers encouragement to prospectors. Any new prospect will get a fair look if there is a chance of a profit.

Greater Lenore President Bob Kasner examining the workings at the Golden Harker property. – G. Kasner

Peter Munk, American Barrick chairman, brought a $40-million gold producer to one with assets of close to $4 billion in nine years. – American Barrick

American Barrick president Robert Smith oversees a mining empire that will produce close to 1.2 million ounces of gold in 1992. – American Barrick

Mac Watson, Freewest president, displays his wares at the Prospectors and Developers Association conference. The gold chocolate bars are a nice touch. – Freewest

JUNIORS AND SENIORS

*"To make money," said Mr. Porteous,
"one must really be interested in money."*

ALDOUS HUXLEY, *ANTIC HAY*

EVERY TIME A NEW MINE HEADFRAME appears on the horizon or an open pit reveals minerals, some mining company has made the significant leap from exploration to production. There are thousands of mining companies in Canada actively looking for economic mineral deposits or promoting promising ground. Few end up as mines. With the high cost of bringing a full plant to production — $60 to $100 million is not uncommon — only large firms have the financial clout to take a proven orebody and deliver gold from it.

Most mining companies are known in the industry as "juniors." Juniors are generally small companies whose main thrust is to obtain claims that have development potential. Financing is usually the biggest problem for such firms. Executives must weigh the importance of the work in the bush against the promotion necessary to win investors. To gain the attention of "seniors," major companies such as Noranda or the Teck Corporation, the small companies must first spend money on their properties. They must strip overburden, do geophysical work, explore the ground and even undertake costly diamond drilling, which, at more than $20 a foot, can easily run into millions of dollars. Very few juniors hold on to their claims. Most hope to sell their properties and obtain royalty payments on minerals extracted.

Greater Lenora Resources is one junior mining company that has survived and prospered. Lenora has been a going concern since 1979 when Bob Kasner gave up a secure job and gambled all he owned to enter the risky business of finding mines. He credits the backing of his wife's small business for a good share of his success. Kasner learned how junior companies presented themselves and placed their properties in the best light. Time spent out in the field with veteran prospectors helped him to understand how to look for surface prospects. He spent all his time out prospecting and studying corporate finance. Greater Lenora has experienced some tough times and disappointments since 1979, but the firm has had some interesting properties. Kasner acquired the Omega, an old Larder Lake mine, and mined out the crown pillar. In order to save cash-strapped Lenora the expense, the milling of recovered ore was done by Balmoral, a larger outfit. Many joint ventures like this occur among juniors.

A 42-cubic-yard shovel loads a 190-ton truck at the Betze Pit, Goldstrike Mine (1991).
– American Barrick Resources Corporation

Bob Kasner's biggest problem is not in finding promising deposits but in maintaining cash flow. Flow-through financing kept many small companies afloat in the mid-eighties. Now presidents of junior companies spend much of their time securing investment funds. Fund-raising depends partly on publicity in order to keep Bob Kasner's business in the public eye and intrigue potential investors. Bob and his brother Glen, field supervisor with Greater Lenora, have prospects across Canada. The claims held are not all gold claims. Right now, excitement centres around a diamond hunt in the Northwest Territories. Stamina, patience and a little luck will give Bob Kasner and Greater Lenora a piece of a new mine.

Freewest Resources president Mackenzie Watson is close to the success that all junior companies seek. Hailed as Prospector of the Year by the Prospectors and Developers Association in 1989, Watson has found a property that is sure to make a mine. Like most others in the business, he served a long apprenticeship before reaching this point. He took a geology degree in New Brunswick and worked as an exploration manager for big firms before branching out on his own. He was involved with another junior company, but realized that he had to a have a large personal stake in a mining company before he would have some degree of security.

Freewest came into being in Montreal, where venture capital is not difficult to raise. Watson has exceptional ability in investor relations. A prospect will not go forward if it cannot be sold. Noranda liked the Freewest approach and farmed out some claims it had east of Matheson for the junior company to investigate. Watson saw the potential at once. The property was astride the Porcupine–Destor Fault, host to many gold producers, and near the Holt–McDermott Mine in Holloway Township. Hemlo Gold Mines joined the Freewest exploration, and the two companies drilled 80,772 metres in 170 holes. Consultants concluded from the drill cores that the reserves on the property held 6.86 million tons of 0.23-grade gold. Miners sit up and take notice of these kinds of figures.

The property was situated partially on the old Teddy Bear Mines ground. After negotiation, interests were apportioned at fifty-one percent to Hemlo Gold, thirty-four percent to Freewest, and fifteen percent to Teddy Bear. The next step was to validate the size of the orebody by underground drilling. The price tag would come to $12 million to sink a shaft 430 metres, do some drifting to access the ore, and take a 5,000-ton bulk sample. The 18-month exploration project was soon under way, to be completed by the fall of 1993. The results of the project confirmed the size of the orebody and bumped the grade up to 0.25. It would mean a capital cost of $60 million to construct a 1,550-ton-per-day operation. This is where a junior company is fortunate to have partners of stature. Freewest will gain 40,000 ounces of gold a year when the new mine is complete. Profits from the operation will fund a gold prospect near Senneterre, Quebec. The company track record should encourage investors to take a position in this successful firm. As for Mac Watson, he is not a miner. "When the Holloway project is in the development stage," he says, "I will be out again looking for new orebodies."

American Barrick Resources Corporation is the top-performing Canadian gold company listed on the Toronto Stock Exchange. In 1991 its total output was 789,846 ounces. Reserves were recently estimated at 25 million ounces. Pete Munk built Barrick into a giant gold company. He made a reputation in the consumer electronics business and later in vacation hotels in the South Pacific. Barrick Petroleum, a small oil and gas firm, became his vehicle to enter the resource business. After changing the name to Barrick Resources, his first purchase was a half interest in Renabie Gold Mine near Wawa, followed by a stake in Camflo Mines near Val d'Or, Quebec.

Peter Munk's business acumen is complemented by the work of Barrick president Bob Smith, who knows where to find gold and dig it out. The former miner from Haileybury and the much-travelled financier both have a flair for hiring talented people. This allows them to let mines operate autonomously while they are taking care of capital projects, finances and budgets. The secret to Barrick's success has been a drive to build up extensive gold reserves while forward-selling all gold production. The properties that gave this miner its start are gone now, but with Holt–McDermott in Ontario and big projects in the United States and South America, the company has close to $4 billion in assets.

In addition to its extensive environmental commitments, the company has a strong sense of community responsibility. One percent of each year's earnings are donated to charity, and each mine has its own fund for assisting the community. Bob Smith feels the staff is the prime reason for the growth of American Barrick Resources; in the past ten years it has become the largest gold miner in North America.

A miner works with a diamond-drill rig underground at the David Bell Mine. — Teck Corp.

DIAMOND DRILLERS

Our crews understand the demands of the contract drilling business.

N. MORISSETTE CANADA INC.

THE SCENE COULD BE a remote part of Northern Canada, perhaps deep in the bush or the high Arctic tundra. With no roads or navigable waterways, the spot would be accessible only by air. The silence of this lonely land is broken by the clatter of helicopter rotors. A machine lands and five men alight. Even as the helicopter curves aloft they make camp and prepare for its return. All day long the airborne link with the south makes return trips to the site with machinery and other supplies slung beneath its skids. The men on the ground have much experience unloading such cargo. Within 48 hours, a prefabricated bunkhouse, cookery, engineer shack, and dry are assembled. Soon the steady hum of a diesel engine accompanies the work that goes on from dawn to dusk. The whirr of a diamond drill can be heard at this camp up to 15 kilometres away. The helicopter flies crews to and from the site at shift changes.

Diamond drillers can be found at work all over the country. Their primary function is to obtain a core of the Earth's crust. The rock core they bring up enables geologists to assess the economic value of a large sample of bedrock. If precious or base metals exist beneath the surface, a planned sequence of drill holes will prove the reserves. Huge financial commitment is necessary to build new mines or extensions to existing ones. Diamond drilling is an efficient method of providing the desired data.

Napoleon Morissette started his diamond-drilling firm in 1926 when he was hired to do underground drilling at the O'Brien Mine in Cobalt. Since that time the Haileybury-based contractor has survived the ups and downs of the economy and business has grown steadily. Today it is both a contractor and manufacturer for the mining industry. There are branches in Ontario, Quebec and Saskatchewan. In 1986 Longyear Canada bought out Morissette and its associated firms, thereby pooling the expertise and resources of both companies while retaining their operating independence.

Morissette lists the location of its drill rigs on a weekly basis. In one recent season there were twenty-seven rigs out in the field. Surface drilling accounts for roughly a quarter of all contracts. In this period they were drilling on surface for three companies across the North. Underground drilling is the firm's bread and butter. Crews were running rigs underground for twelve mining outfits at twelve locations spread over half of Canada. With a drill consultant based in Africa and a busy technical testing area in Cobalt, Morissette bits are always boring into the ground somewhere. Morissette maintains its high output in the field with an average of 745,582 metres drilled per year.

The head office is situated on a bluff at Haileybury overlooking Lake Temiskaming. The white-sided building doubles as an industrial plant. Large overhead doors along the side provide entry to machine-servicing shops and outside, drill shacks await delivery to a new operating location. This building provides drillers with drills, power packs, controls, tools, and rods as well as all food supplies. In the quiet foyer a refurbished early drill and statues of a claim staker and gold panner are on display. A framed statement of purpose affirming the company's commitment to service is entitled "Morissette Core Values."

The operations manager checks out the ground before the firm bids on a job. Field supervisors assess accessibility of the terrain, water sources, equipment needs, and any special circumstances. On-site examination data enables the contract manager to cost the job, add the profit margin, and come up with a competitive price. Not long after such a bid, surface or underground drilling begins.

Morissette has pioneered wireline drilling since it was introduced in the early sixties. The original principle stays the same. A power unit rotates the core barrel. At the end of the barrel is a reaming shell, set with industrial diamonds. Screwed into the shell is a drill bit with more diamonds either surface-set or impregnated in the steel, depending on the requirements of the job. Drill firms keep track of these bits, as they can run from $125 to $1,000 each depending on their size (from 48 mm to 96 mm in diameter). A typical bit may last for 150 metres of hardrock drilling before it must be exchanged. Water is pumped through the rods to cool the bit and flush out rock chips. In wireline drilling, an inside tube holding the core can be detached and pulled to surface by means of a wire dropped down the drill rods. The tube is then returned down the core barrel, and drilling resumes. Thus, since the entire rods do not have to be pulled, drilling time is sped up, there is less wear and tear on the drill, and operator fatigue is lessened.

Most drills are hydraulic and are run by diesel or electric motors. All drill equipment is set up for easy transport. One particular power pack being readied for a Northern job was on skids, had slots for a forklift and slings for a helicopter and even came with a set of wheels in case it had to be tracked underground.

In their 8- to 12-hour shifts, drill runners and helpers must apply the skills of various trades. Drillers are handy at wiring, carpentry, plumbing, simple mechanics, hydraulics and instrument reading, plus the operation of heavy equipment such as tractors, skidders and a variety of tracked vehicles. Such workers must be self-motivated, as they often work in isolation without close supervision.

When customers require on-target drilling, the dip and azimuth of the drilled hole must be controlled. This is done by turning the bit and thrusting the rods rather than rotating them. The amount of thrust and distance drilled keeps the hole in line. When a second directional hole is required from an existing one, a tapered wedge is used to deflect the drill string in the preferred direction. The firm designs its own wedges for specific jobs. Wedging techniques are especially helpful in obtaining deep, flat holes. This work requires first-rate drillers and top-notch equipment because horsepower has to be monitored carefully and proper water flows maintained.

Working mines use diamond-drill services continually to both operate and test rock strength. The latter is done by over-coring. A deep, narrow hole is drilled and a sensing device is placed in it. The device is monitored while the same hole is redrilled with a larger bit. Ground support for underground workings is made easier with the drills. In tie-back drilling, a hole is drilled and cement holds a cable set within it. The cable is tensed and then more cement finishes the job. A large area of the rock roof can be supported in this manner. Morissette also drills large holes for exploration, assists water control by putting down drain holes, and provides passages for electric cables. Holes are checked carefully for rock caving and water seepage. Not all drilling is done for the mining industry. The firm has done much soil testing — even testing the permeability of bedrock for the possible storage of radioactive materials.

Morissette assists the Haileybury School of Mines in operating a practical teaching centre for its diamond-drill school. This facility sits in a former silver mine near Cobalt. The Meteor adit of the old Silverfields Mine runs straight through the base of a hillside to a large raise mined in the twenties. Old mine-shaft timbers and a ropeless sheave-wheel remain in the excavation as a testimony to a time when the mine operated from this level down to two stations below. Now the place that was hidden for perhaps half a century does service again. In one section of the adit, a compact LM 22 diamond drill gives students practice in operation. Over in the raise, a large LM 75 machine is set up to drill into the face. Both machines give practice in field drilling conditions. The pump draws water from the old submerged shaft, and the operation is relatively quiet. When graduates of this program enter the work force, employers will recognize valid experience in underground drilling.

Morissette president Dare Fowler runs a company that has been in a specialized business for a long time and has maintained a lead in technology. In this demanding service industry, reputation is probably the most valuable asset.

Assayers in the early days of the Porcupine camp had rough-and-ready accommodations. – OA S8241

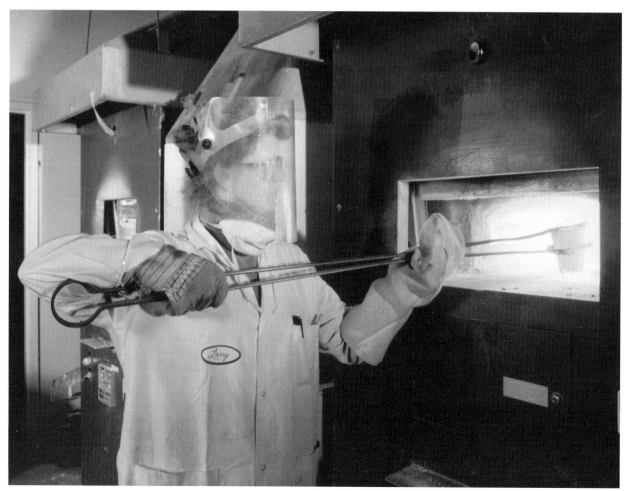

A technician removes fired assay pots from the Williams Mine refinery furnace. – Teck Corp.

ASSAYER

*I have appointed you an assayer of my people;
you will test them and assay their conduct.*

JEREMIAH 6: 27–30

MODERN ASSAY LABORATORY takes rock chips (or drill-core shards) and analyzes and processes them. A jaw crusher, working at a dull roar, renders the sample down to a mix of granules and small chips. The specimen is then pulverized — reduced to a fine powder. Silica sand is kept handy for cleaning out the pulverizer so that the next sample will not be contaminated. Matting is the final stage in sample preparation. Once the fine powdery material is tumbled on a rubber mat it is ready for its test by fire.

The prepped material is neatly sorted into envelopes and weighed in a glass-enclosed balance scale. The traditional beam balances are gone now, as the new scales are faster and can stand more wear. Each weighed sample then goes into a fire assay pot, a 20-gram crucible about the size of a foam coffee cup. The pot is loaded with a lead-based flux. The mix contains lead oxide, soda ash, borax and sometimes even a pinch of flour. After a spot of silver nitrate is added, the contents of the pot show as a green and white powder with a blob of silver.

The gas furnace holds up to thirty-six pots. The door slides up and a rectangle of white heat appears in the opening. Pots are placed in the chamber with a long fork, arranged in the same order as they were on the rack in order to keep track of the contents. After the door clangs shut the samples receive a searing 1,050°C heat for 40 minutes. The flux melts in each pot and a lead metal is formed by a rolling action. Any precious metal present is dissolved in the lead. When the pots are forked out of the fire, the residue in them is a red-hot molten mass. This is poured into a cast-iron button-mould tray shaped somewhat like a muffin tin. The fire-tested materials cool quickly. The lead sinks to the bottom and green slag remains on top. The hardened samples are hammered to separate the lead buttons from the slag, and then the buttons are placed in cupels (tiny white vessels made of magnesium cement). Old-timers used cupels made of bone ash, more commonly used in the production of bone china, but the magnesium version is much less expensive. Another 40 minutes of fire, this time in the electric furnace, and the cupel obligingly soaks up the lead, leaving a silver dore bead at the bottom of the vessel. As for the lead-laden cupels, they are donated to local mines, which use the metal in mill circuits.

Except for some high-tech equipment, the process of fire assaying has not changed in hundreds of years. Assayers in the times of the great gold rushes would place the silver bead in a "parting cup," a tiny glazed ceramic vessel. A few drops of nitric acid dissolve the silver. Any gold left behind appears as a black, spongelike material. The gold is washed and dried and placed for a minute or so in the furnace. It emerges as a tiny bead, often so small it requires a magnifying glass to see it. The early assayers would carefully weigh this product in order to calculate the grade.

Modern assayers still use this procedure for gold bullion or samples rich in the precious metal. For lower grades they use a more modern method. Nitric acid of a higher concentration is used to dissolve the silver. The gold is then dissolved by adding a solution of concentrated hydrochloric acid to form aqua regia or "royal water." A test tube full of this solution is then subjected to the most precise measuring device available, an atomic absorption spectrophotometer (A.A.S.). This computer-controlled instrument is programmed to measure gold standards. A flame fed by an air-acetylene blend is ignited in the chamber next to the computer. A tiny tube sucks up the gold in solution and the flame changes as the liquid is vaporized. Set in the lamp housing of the A.A.S. is a gold lamp, which has a coating of the precious metal within its core. The light from the lamp interacts with the gold atoms in the flame and the instrument reads the results. The measurement is so accurate that the gold in the solution can be detected in amounts as small as 0.0005 ounces to the ton. All that remains is to issue a certificate of analysis indicating the gold content of the sample.

A large mine milling 5,000 tons a day might perform as many as 750 assays in the same amount of time on samples taken from various operations in the mining and milling process. Gold is almost always contaminated with other metals — most commonly silver. Pure gold is a product of extensive refining. Most operating mines have their own assay departments, but some exploration firms and other organizations use independent assay laboratories to have the work done. The mines will occasionally check the work of their own assayers by using the services of a private lab. The biggest independant assaying company in Northern Ontario is Accurassay, located in Thunder Bay and Kirkland Lake.

Accurassay's president, George Duncan, has a doctorate in analytic chemistry. Designed by Duncan, the fire assay area is a series of small rooms covering 102 square metres. All doors are kept closed in this area to avoid contamination of samples by unrelated materials. Attention to detail and confidentiality are very important in all aspects of assaying, as mining companies decide to whether to proceed with major capital investment in mineral extraction based on assay results.

One problem in mining — highlighted recently by independent laboratories such as Accurassay — has been the "nugget effect." Gold distribution in ore samples is almost always uneven, and the precious metal in the sample may not give a representative assay. The nugget effect appears when fire assay samples are small relative to the amount of bulk material examined. The larger the sample the less the chance of a fundamental error in analysis. Cyanide leaching is one way of providing accurate samples. In this method, the sample is tumbled for several hours in a hot cyanide solution to dissolve the gold. The solution is then analysed for gold content and the residues are assayed. Such results are found to be highly accurate.

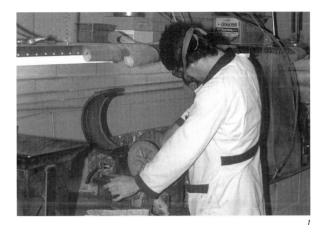

2

1

3

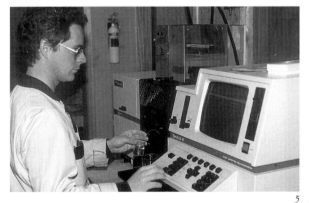

5

1. *Crushed mineral samples are pulverized before being assayed.*

2. *Crucibles loaded with flux and mineral samples await their turn in the gas furnace.*

3. *A charge of thirty-six crucibles awaits removal from the furnace. The molten contents will be poured into cupels (right) for a further trial by fire.*

4. *Removal of crucibles from the furnace.*

5. *A technician operates the atomic absorption spectrophotometer. His left hand holds the tube that feeds aqua regia to the fire chamber.* – Accurassay

Accurassay performs assays on silver, platinum, palladium and base metals as well as on gold. Traditionally, assaying was considered a trade and labs did not use chemists in their operation. This limited technological advancement, as the process was performed according to custom rather than understanding. Today the full-service facility is managed by chemists. The environmental work done for mines and other customers often exceeds that done by the firm's assay department. Whereas in fire assaying, single tests are done on a large number of samples, in environmental testing, a few samples are often subjected to a wide variety of tests. Much of the work in this field is done on waters to check for the presence of toxic contaminants, which have the potential to harm the environment. The layperson visiting an environmental laboratory finds a bewildering array of sophisticated testing equipment for a variety of potential safety hazards.

The Mint refinery (1938) could easily be mistaken for an old country castle by visitors to Ottawa.
– Royal Canadian Mint

This drab room housed the chlorination furnaces (left) and tilting furnaces (right) of the Mint (1936).
– PA 132085

THE
ROYAL CANADIAN MINT

*Money is such as a sixth sense without which
you cannot make a complete use of the other five.*

W. SOMERSET MAUGHAM

SUSSEX DRIVE is one of the most prestigious thoroughfares in Canada. The official residence of the prime minister is on it, and across the way stands Rideau Hall, home to the governor general. Visitors who turn onto Sussex Drive from downtown Ottawa pass the Canadian War Museum. Nearby, an imposing Tudor-style sandstone building stands high above the Ottawa River. An elegant wrought-iron fence surrounds the place. There is a guard house on the corner. The overall effect of this structure is one of calm and security — and that is how it should be at the headquarters of the Royal Canadian Mint.

Few Canadians realize that behind the calm Tudor facade sits the largest gold refinery in the Western hemisphere — the third-largest after South Africa and the former U.S.S.R. The refinery is located in the north end of the building. Few of the people who work elsewhere in the plant, or the close to 60,000 tourists who visit the Mint annually, have been in the refinery.

Canada ranks fifth in world gold production after South Africa, the United States, the former U.S.S.R. and Australia. Roughly seventy percent of all gold mined in Canada is refined at the Royal Canadian Mint. In 1991 that came to a handsome 4.75 million troy ounces. Customers have also brought gold for processing from South America, the United States and the Pacific Rim.

The Mint offers its customers absolute security. Incoming gold is transported by armoured carrier in the form of dore bars. The bars are approximately eighty percent gold, with some silver and base metals. They are stored in the mine containers, some in wooden boxes, others in cardboard or sacking, while a few even travel in old military munition boxes.

In the refinery, the rough gold is first melted in an electric induction furnace in order that uniform samples may be taken for assaying. The dore bars contain different percentages of gold, depending on the quality of preliminary smelting at the mines. Once the gold content is determined, chlorine gas is injected into the molten mass. The chlorine gas binds with the silver and base metals in the mix, but the injection is stopped before the gold is chemically bound. Some of the resulting base metals are picked up in the ventilator system and collected by an electric precipitator. The remaining molten silver and base metals are skimmed off the top of the mix for later purification. The gold in the crucible now assays at 99.5 percent. This is further refined in an electrolytic process to 99.99 percent, the finest quality obtainable. The end product is a spongelike material that is cast into bars.

Gold bars are available in several sizes, including 100-ounce, 400-ounce and kilo bars. Gold is also sold in granular form to the electronics and jewellery industries. The high-security vault is a drab functional storage place, but the riches it contains make the area come alive with a warm yellow glow. The gold, stamped with the hallmark of the Royal Canadian Mint, remains secure pending delivery instructions by the owner.

Canada identified a need to produce its own coinage as early as 1901. Gold was being produced in the Yukon and British Columbia, and at the time it was being exported to the United States for refining. It was believed that a mint could refine gold in Canada and produce British gold sovereigns. The Ottawa branch of the Royal Mint was established after lengthy negotiations, and the first coin was struck on January 2, 1908. Britain retained control until 1931 when the Royal Canadian Mint came into being. Over three decades later, in 1969, it became a federal Crown corporation. Through an amendment to the Royal Canadian Mint Act in 1989, the Ministry of Supply and Services purchased shares in the Mint. The move has been profitable for the shareholder. Since 1969 the Royal Canadian Mint has paid $150 million into the Consolidated Revenue Fund.

The handsome building on Sussex Drive had major additions in 1935 and 1952. Some space was gained when circulation coinage production moved to a new plant

Electrolytic cells for refining fine gold at the Ottawa refinery. – Alain Cornu, Royal Canadian Mint

Pouring coinage bars at the mint (1940).
– Public Archives Canada

in Winnipeg in 1975. However, there was still not enough space to accommodate the expanding organization. Commercial space was rented in Vanier and industrial quarters in Hull. An engineering study in 1978 confirmed that all activities could be housed under one roof, and the 1908 building was completely renovated. The facade of the building was protected by the Ontario Heritage Act. The Mint exterior would survive as part of the nation's history and the central location remained as a tourist attraction. The renovation, begun in 1984, took two years to complete. The fine windows, railings, mouldings and even a fireplace were restored to their original splendour.

Visitors touring the Mint pay a small entrance fee to cover operating expenses of the tour. They enter through the elegant vaulted lobby and assemble in the Green Room where they find a display of historic and contemporary coins as well as a souvenir shop. New uncirculated rolls of coins are a popular item. A film highlights the Mint's role and products. The tour that follows illustrates the many aspects of coin minting. No more than 1,400 coins are produced on an average eight-hour shift in order to maintain the high standard for gold coins. The presses can operate at a much higher speed. The presses at the Winnipeg plant, for example, strike 100,000 circulation coins per shift. Coins may have a plain, serrated or lettered edge, and may be shaped or round.

The gold destined for coinage is cast in a bar 125 mm wide, 60 mm long, and 40 mm thick. The bar becomes thicker and longer as it passes through the rolls on the finishing mill to meet the required specifications. The strip is passed through a blanking press where the round coin blank is cut from the strip. White-gloved operators examine the cut blanks and reject those that do not meet the specification. Next the blanks receive a raised edge in an operation called rimming. They are then annealed, or softened, in a computer-controlled annealing furnace. These prepared blanks are washed and burnished to ensure that the surface is as clean as possible. Just prior to striking, the blanks are degreased again and then they are minted in the Graebner presses.

Both obverse and reverse dies are impressed simultaneously and the result is the finest level of the minter's craft. Even though the coins are weighed before striking, they are checked twice on completion. First, an operator uses a scale to record the weight. Next, a robot takes the coins and places them in trays, judging which ones meet the specified weight and separating them from those not up to par. Rejects will go back to the refinery for recycling. The fine coins are carefully packed before being transferred to the shipping area. Bullion and numismatic coins are placed in packages to protect the valuable contents. Even as they are being packaged, the coins are examined to see if any imperfect specimens have survived all the rigorous testing.

While much is made of the refinery and the gold products that come from it, the Mint's primary function is less glamorous but no less vital to the nation's well-being. The Mint is mandated to produce and arrange for the supply of circulation coinage for the Canadian monetary system. This operation at the Winnipeg plant provides a tremendous boost to the country's copper and nickel mines. The ultra-modern facility has an annual capacity of over two billion coins. The new national coinage distribution system, instituted in 1989, has improved the recirculation of coins within the network, thereby reducing the need for new coins.

The Maple Leaf gold coin is the most popular of all gold coinage in the world. – Royal Canadian Mint

James C. Corkery, former master and now chairman of the Mint board, holds fine gold products of the refinery. Note the rough bars behind him, as received from the mines. – Photo Features

In 1991 the Mint held a competition inviting all Canadians to submit designs for the celebration of 125th anniversary of Confederation. A panel of judges reviewed all 11,003 entries and selected those that best captured the essence of the provinces and territories. Twenty-five-cent coins feature provincial scenes such as the Kluane National Park in the Yukon and Alberta's hoodoos. In addition, a special one-dollar coin was struck in honour of the anniversary. It features children proudly saluting the Parliament buildings.

Since 1976 the Winnipeg plant has produced coins in more than forty denominations for several foreign clients. The mint averages a yearly production of 500 million coins — more coins for more countries than any other private or national mint. Progress has been made in securing these foreign contracts by offering nickel-bonded or stainless steel compositions rather than the more expensive copper and nickel-based alloys. The mint also advises other countries on many aspects of coinage. Other products include tokens for souvenirs, advertising and transportation, as well as trade dollars to mark a variety of occasions. Governments, universities and private businesses have all made use of the Canadian Mint.

The Mint is business oriented and profit driven. It has been honoured by the Prime Minister with the coveted Canada Export Award in 1986. Aggressive marketing has made the fine numismatic and bullion coins known around the world. Collector coins attract art lovers. The platinum snowy-owl set was designed by Glen Loates, and another wildlife theme was created by Robert Bateman. In 1991, a 22-carat gold coin featured children playing hockey, and an aviation series of 24-carat gold-covered silver coins featured cameos of famous flyers. Since 1990 a new likeness of the queen has been used. It is the first image of a reigning monarch designed by a Canadian artist — Dora de Pedery-Hunt.

Of all the coins produced at the Royal Canadian Mint, the gold Maple Leaf is struck the most. Great care is taken in the manufacture of these coins. The price fixed according to current precious-metal values. The gold Maple Leaf coins are among the most popular bullion coins in the world. They are authorized by the Government of Canada and are 99.99 percent pure gold. Such items are easily traded, act as a hedge against inflation, and are both profitable and easy to store. Unlike numismatic coins, which are struck in limited quantity and sold at significant premium, the bullion coin is acquired for the intrinsic value of the metal. These coins, with the queen on one side and the maple leaf on the other, is especially popular in Asian countries. It projects a good image of Canada and boosts the balance of payments while providing a ready market for Canadian gold mines. Since its introduction in 1979, the gold Maple Leaf has sold over 14.6 million ounces of Canadian-mined gold.

The Royal Canadian Mint began to seek new sources of revenue when it became a Crown corporation in 1969. Today it stands out among world mints for its diversity of products and its technical expertise. The corporation is a good moneymaker for its shareholders — the Canadian people.

When it reaches 1,100°C, 99.99 percent pure gold is poured into bars and ingots of various size for customers all over the world. – Royal Canadian Mint

WORKER IN GOLD

Go for gold.

USA OLYMPIC SLOGAN, 1980

PURE GOLD is said to be of 24-carat standard. This means that 999.99 parts per thousand are gold. Carat comes from the Italian *carato,* the Arabic *qirat* and the Greek *keration,* all meaning "the fruit of the carob tree." The hornlike pods of this tree contain seeds that were once used to balance precious-metal scales in Oriental bazaars.

Since 24-carat gold is too soft for jewellery, the metal is often alloyed with other metals such as silver, copper and zinc. The highest standard is usually 22-carat (916 parts per thousand). This was common years ago, but price considerations have made 18-carat more common for jewellery, especially when set with diamonds. Many gold chains sold in shopping malls and department stores are within the 9- to 10-carat range.

Twenty-two-carat gold is favoured in Asia and the Middle East. Hallmarks indicating the maker's initial, metal quality, assay and year are punched into the gold. Since gold can be white, pink, grey, blue or green, depending on the metals it is alloyed with it, these proofs are very important. Advertising claims of "pure gold," "solid-gold ore," and even "solid 10-carat-gold plated" are often misleading or just do not make sense. The problem of recognition for the purchaser can be further compounded when a piece of jewellery is gold in colour but has a silver hallmark, which means it has been gold-plated after hallmarking. Most people in the trade agree that it is important to deal with a reputable jeweller.

Most jewellery stores today are primarily sales places and rarely have a trained craftsman on staff. The expression "we'll have to send it away" is thus commonplace. The true jeweller is one who can produce one-of-a-kind pieces. Christof Weidner is one such jeweller. He is an exception to the growing concentration of commercial craftsmen in big-city firms. He creates his original pieces in South Porcupine, a suburb of Timmins. Weidner served a four-year apprenticeship in his native Austria, where he had a mixture of classroom study and practical experience. The budding goldsmith worked as a helper at first. His early design instruction was in brass and silver. These mediums are relatively inexpensive and lend themselves to the learning process. Some students find their métier in silver for the religious market, fashioning chalices and other sacramental pieces. Weidner went on to learn the capabilities of the more-prized metal. Much hinges on the smithing

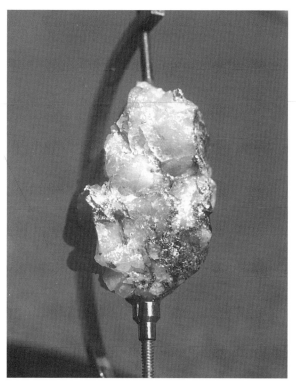

Gold in quartz from the Dome Mine. – C. Weidner

A gold nugget brooch by Christof Weidner. – C. Weidner

process, in which the gold is beaten out in fine sheets for later work. Only through practice can the potential of the malleable metal be achieved. By the time Weidner graduated and reached the close of his apprenticeship, he was working at the top level of the trade.

To broaden his knowledge, Weidner spent time working in Switzerland, where the output and quality of fine jewellery is closely monitored by a regulatory body. The first of three Swiss firms he worked for employed him in repairs. This gave him the chance to study the work of craftsmen from all over Europe. He finally spent time in fine hand-work, making crowns and individual settings for rings.

Weidner emigrated to Canada to learn more about jewellery in a new setting. Within three days of arriving in Montreal, he had a job. He was employed making original pieces in the workroom of an exclusive store. Once he had saved some money, the young craftsman went to work for himself. He made a display case, filled it with original items and then sold directly to the trade. The newcomer was once robbed of all the pieces in his display case, but he started again, working until he could leave the city. He took advantage of the scarcity of trained jewellers in small-town Ontario.

Weidner has a store in the Porcupine Mall. He works at the counter but when the pace slackens he is off to the rear workshop to design and make his unique jewellery. The stations along his workbench have semi-circles cut out of the counter, below which are pull-out drawers lined with tin. These are meant to catch stray particles of gold. It is a common rule in the trade to watch out for gold that may be otherwise lost in pouring the metal, polishing, buffing or washing. Collected in dust and solution, the valuable waste can be reclaimed.

Special-order pieces and those made for speculation are highly personalized. One mining company wants a number of gold tiepins to reward employees for long-time safety records. First Weidner designs an original tiepin, cutting the intricate design from a sheet of silver. The finished piece is used to fabricate rubber moulds. Next a "jewel" tree is set up. Moulds are grafted onto this stick of wax on a stand, and then it is placed in a canister and filled with plaster of Paris to hold it firm for the next stage. When the unit is heated to 700°C, the wax is burned off and molten gold is injected into the space that is left, using either vacuum or centrifuge methods. The finished gold items are perfectly formed. After polishing and buffing the pins, Weidner rounds off his work by dotting an 'i' in the distinctive company logo with a small diamond.

Weidner's popularity derives from his novel approach, which draws clients from across the continent. He uses gold purchased from local mines that is still imbedded in milky quartz. Much care must be taken to separate the gold from the quartz. Some workers use acid, but Weidner feels this is a crude method of extraction, as it is potentially dangerous to the worker and is unnecessarily complicated. He picks up a small chunk. Holding the piece with tongs over a water jar, he fires up his fine-nozzle oxygen-propane torch and gently probes all facets of the rock with the fine flame. As the intense heat plays upon the quartz, the host rock seems to shrink and tiny flakes of quartz fall into the water. Occasionally the flame is put aside in favour of a dental pick to root out quartz tucked away in crevices of the gold. Within a few minutes a small nugget is revealed. Stripped of the bland quartz, the yellow nugget is twisted and turned in various directions for the first time since it was formed thousands of years earlier. Care in extraction means the difference between separate gold flakes and a whole nugget. The price of the nugget is determined by the gold content, the work involved and the artistic merit of the item. One huge nugget, roughly the size and shape of an egg, is kept in a simple washcloth bag. The scales show this dazzling piece to be 4.1 troy ounces. Through the jeweller's glass, the rare nugget is breathtakingly beautiful. Light catches the lustrous precious metal from every angle. Such a piece will perhaps end up on a pedestal or set in fine crystal in a museum or private collection.

Scattered around the smith's small workshop are the tools of the trade and the material shaped by them. Diamonds wait to be placed in settings, and gold buttons and scraps are plentiful. Handmade rings await nuggets or gems to make them complete. The jeweller will not commence a commissioned piece until he is certain of the buyer's preferences. As he sits surrounded by beautiful items that represent the dreams of others, Weidner talks of his own hopes. One day he would like to work only in gold and put together a group of craftsmen who would create fine jewellery that is distinctively Northern.

His special creations are kept in the safe, waiting to be displayed to serious shoppers. Earrings of tiny nuggets, pendants with leaf gold and some specimen rings grace one display case. There is even a tray of nuggets. Customers can pick one and then decide how it should be mounted.

In the meantime, Weidner is anxious to get back to the workshop. There are so many fine gold items to craft.

1. In June 1989, the steamer **Majestic** brought thirty members of the legislature and seventeen reporters to view the gold camp around Mine Centre.   – OA 10399 23

2. Miners at an unknown Elk Lake property gather in front of the cookhouse.   – OA6920 S12677

3. Summer accommodations at the Shenango Mine, 1936.   – John Larche Collection

4. Shenango Mine manager Jack Owens and A. Buisson used a motor rail car to transport supplies to Oba.   – Pa 14862

5. David Bell, Teck president Norman Keevil, John Larche and Don McKinnon in the headframe at the David Bell Mine.   – John Larche Collection

6. Native security guard at the Musselwhite project, north of Sioux Lookout.   – Placer Dome

AN ONTARIO
GOLD CHRONOLOGY

1849 Small quantities of gold discovered during copper mining at Bruce Mines.

1866 Gold discovered on the Richardson farm near Madoc, the first lode-gold found in the Precambrian Shield. It caused great excitement, but only 85 ounces were said to have been produced.

1868 Ontario enacted the Gold and Silver Act, which set up mining divisions and a system for staking claims and issuing miners' licences.

1869 Ontario passed the General Mining Act, under which mining locations could be sold by the acre without special requirements as to the discovery of a deposit or a commitment to operate.

1871 The first discovery of gold in Northwestern Ontario at the Moss Mine (later the Huronian).

1872 Gold discovered in various locations in the Lake of the Woods area of Northwestern Ontario.

1882 Ontario introduced a mining royalty tax.

1890 Gold rush in Northwestern Ontario, with Wendigo, Mikado, Sultana and Regina as the chief properties.

1892 Discovery of the Ophir Mine in Galbraith Township east of Sault Ste. Marie.

1895 Gold discovered on the north shore of Lake Superior at Jackfish and Schreiber.

1897 Gold discovered at Michipicoten.

1898 Border dispute between Ontario and Manitoba, which had held up development of the Lake of the Woods and Seine River gold areas, was decided by Privy Council in favour of Ontario.

1903 Silver discovered at Cobalt, spurring discovery of the great Northeastern Ontario gold camps. Opening of the Laurentian Mine south of Dryden was the beginning of a small gold camp.

1906 Abitibi and Larder Lake gold areas discovered.

1907 As gold traded at $17.43 U.S. an ounce, mining of the metal in Southern Ontario was felt to be a risky venture. Gold first discovered in the Porcupine on Gold Island in Night Hawk Lake.

1908 Gold discovered at Painkiller Lake, Matheson.

1909 Porcupine gold rush started with the discovery of the Dome property.

1911–1912 Gold discovered between Swastika and Kirkland Lake and also to the west at Shining Tree.

1914 As gold was discovered at Boston Creek in Northeastern Ontario, the province was acclaimed as the principal source of the metal in Canada. Unfortunately the price of gold was unchanged from its declared value in 1717 due to world oversupply. The Gold Standard was suspended due to the First World War, and the price proved erratic for the next 20 years.

1918 Gold discovered near Goudreau close by the Algoma Central Railway.

1920 Ontario produced seventy-four percent of the gold in Canada.

1924 The Timmins Hollinger Mine was the biggest gold mine in Canada.

1925 Gold discovered at Red Lake.

1928 Gold discovered at Pickle Lake.

1929 The stock market crash strengthened gold prospects.

1931 Gold discovered in the Geraldton–Beardmore area of Northwestern Ontario.

1934 The United States fixed the price of gold at $35 U.S. an ounce, and gold exploration increased in Ontario.

1936 Gold mines were given a tax exemption to encourage development in Canada, and the Pamour Mine of South Porcupine was the first new property to qualify.

1939 Ontario gold mines prospered when the precious metal was used to obtain U.S. dollars for the purchase of war materials.

1942 Gold mines slumped when gold was declared a non-war industry and restrictions were placed on labour and supplies.

1948 The Emergency Gold Measures Act (E.G.M.A.) enabled Canadian gold mines to compete on the world market. The only mine that did not require assistance was Campbell Red Lake, which milled 200,000 ounces a year after 1949.

1960 Increased costs caused many Ontario gold mines to close.

1970 Gold fell to $33 U.S. an ounce, causing marginal mines to close.

1971 Gold became freely convertible and rose to $38 U.S. an ounce.

1973 The precious metal reached $100 U.S. an ounce.

1974 Gold discovered at Detour Lake in Northwestern Ontario.

1976 The E.G.M.A. was terminated.

1978 Gold reached $200 U.S. an ounce.

1979 Gold climbed to $400 U.S. an ounce.

1980 Gold price peaked at $800 an ounce and settled back to the $500 to $600 range.

1983 Canadian gold developers received an "earned depletion" allowance for tax purposes of one-and-one-third times the amount spent on exploration and development. This encouraged production and became known as flow-through financing.

1987 Gold reached $640 U.S. an ounce.

1989 Flow-through financing was removed.

1990 There was a considerable drop in exploration and development of gold prospects in Ontario. Since that time a minimum of $400 per ounce has been seen as necessary to encourage future exploration and development.

MINING TERMS

ADIT: An opening driven horizontally into the side of a hill or mountain to provide access to a mineral deposit. A tunnel is open at both ends, while an adit is only open at one.

ANOMALY: Any departure from the norm that may indicate the presence of minerals in the bedrock.

ASSAY: A chemical test performed on mineral samples to determine the amount of minerals contained within them.

ASSESSMENT WORK: The activity specified by law that must be done each year to retain legal control of claims. In Ontario, after the first year of staking, work to the value of $400 must be done each year until the province issues a lease.

BACKFILL: Waste rock used to fill a mined-out area.

BEDROCK: The rock forming the earth's crust.

BLASTER: Miner responsible for loading, priming and detonating explosives.

BREAK: A large shear-zone or structural fault.

BULLION: Precious metal in bars or ingots.

CAGE: Conveyance used to transport miners and equipment in a shaft.

CARBON-IN-PULP: Method of recovering gold from cyanide solution by absorbing the metal to granules of activated carbon.

CHANNEL SAMPLE: Sample composed of material taken from a small trench or rock cut.

CLAIM: A portion of land held under federal or provincial law. Claims are 40 acres or 400 metres by 400 metres and can be staked singly or in blocks. A prospector's licence costs $25 and is issued to persons over 18 years of age for a period of five years. All details are found in any Mining Recorder's Office.

COLLAR: Timber or concrete around the mouth of a mine shaft.

CONCENTRATE: Powdery mill product from which waste rock has been removed.

CORE: Cylindrical piece of rock obtained by diamond drilling.

COUNTRY ROCK: Also known as host rock, it is the general mass of rock around which an orebody is found.

CROWN PILLAR: A solid block of ore left near the surface of a mine to provide a roof, preventing caving of the surface plant area.

CUT-AND-FILL: Method of stoping in which ore is removed in slices or lifts. The excavation is filled with waste rock or backfill before the next slice is removed.

DEVELOPMENT: Underground work carried out for the purpose of opening up a mineral deposit.

DIAMOND DRILL: Rotary drill in which the cutting is done by abrasion. The cutting bit is set with industrial diamonds and is attached to long, hollow rods through which water is pumped. The core of the rock is cylindrical and can be removed in sections.

DILUTION: The removal of low grade rock to improve the grade of ore.

DIP: Angle at which a vein or rock is inclined from the horizontal as measured at right angles to the strike.

DORE BAR: Product of a gold or silver mine, usually a mix of gold and silver.

DRIFT: A horizontal opening that follows the vein or rock formation.

DRY: A building where miners change and store clothes.

EXPLORATION: Prospecting, mapping, sampling and drilling for ore.

FACE: The point to which underground mining has progressed.

FLOAT: Rocks that have broken away from a main body and moved some distance away, usually by glacial action.

GEOLOGY: The science of the Earth's crust, its strata and their relation and changes.

GEOPHYSICAL SURVEY: Scientific measurement of physical properties (e.g., magnetism, specific gravity, electrical conductivity and radioactivity) of rocks.

GLORY HOLE: An open-pit mine.

GOLD: Gold is an element (Au). It comes in thin or massive plates. It has a hardness of 2.5 to 3.0 on a scale of 1 to 10 and its specific gravity runs between 15.6 and 19.3. Gold is yellow in colour. It is extremely heavy and very malleable.

GOLD BRICK: A gold brick generally weighs 35 kilograms (77 lb.) and contains close to 1,000 troy ounces.

GRAB SAMPLE: A sample of material taken at random to determine mineral content.

GRUBSTAKE: Funds to back a prospector in return for an interest in any discoveries.

HEADFRAME: The framework on the surface above a shaft that supports the hoisting cables. When sheathed in it becomes a shafthouse.

HOIST: The machine used for raising and lowering the cage.

HIGH-GRADE: Rich ore. A high-grader steals such ore.

IGNEOUS ROCKS: Rocks formed by the solidification of molten material from deep within the Earth.

LEVEL: Horizontal openings underground in a mine.

MANWAY: Passage for miners to travel via stairs or ladder that can be used in an emergency to exit to surface.

METALLURGY: The process of extracting metals from their ores.

MILL: Plant where ore is treated to recover metals in a smaller volume for shipment to a smelter or refinery. A mill can also be part of the crushing machinery.

MINE: An underground plant that extracts desired minerals. A mine is like a factory in a small town. Underground there are roads, lunchrooms, repair rooms, storage areas, waste-water systems and places for people to work. An average mine will have many kilometres of roads (drifts and crosscuts) and stairways (raises) connecting levels. Fresh air is pumped through the mine to maintain healthy working conditions. All equipment and materials must be brought into the mine down a shaft or a spiral roadway.

MINERAL: An inorganic, naturally occurring solid substance of definite chemical composition with definite crystal structure (e.g., quartz, felsdpar, gold, etc.) obtained by mining.

MUCK: Ore that has been broken up by blasting. The name gives no indication of value.

ORE: Mixture of materials and waste from which a metal can be extracted at a profit.

PILLAR: A block of ore or rock left in place to structurally support the shaft, walls or roof in a mine.

PLACER: Alluvial deposit of sand and gravel containing valuable metals.

PROSPECT: A mining property that has not been proved by exploration.

QUARTZ: A mineral, massive or crystalline, in hexagonal prisms.

RAISE: A vertical or inclined underground working that has been excavated from the bottom up.

REFRACTORY ORE: Ore that does not respond to conventional mineral processing.

ROCK: A mass of mineral matter of various composition consolidated in nature by the action of heat, water, air or ice to form part of the Earth's crust.

SALTING: Introducing metals or minerals into samples, resulting in false assays either deliberately or by accident.

SCALING: Removing loose rock from the walls and roof of an underground opening.

SHAFT: Vertical or inclined opening in rock for the purpose of providing access to an orebody.

SHEAVE WHEEL: A grooved wheel at the top of a headframe over which the hoisting rope passes.

SHRINKAGE STOPING: A method of mining whereby part of the broken ore is used as a working platform and as a support for the walls of the stope.

SKIP: A self-dumping bucket used in a shaft to hoist ore or rock.

STATION: A large area in a mine where a level meets a shaft. It is used mainly for storage and equipment handling.

STOPE: An underground excavation where miners work at extracting ore.

TAILINGS: Material rejected from a mill after the valuable minerals are removed. Tailings are often a sandlike substance referred to as "slimes."

THROUGH THE MILL: In mining this means the product has been crushed, screened, floated, dewatered, aerated, agitated, thickened, clarified, filtered and heated in a furnace.

VEIN: A fissure in rock that is filled with minerals deposited through volcanic action from deep underground.

WINZE: This is similar to the hoist for a shaft, but a hoist is at surface and a winze is located underground.

An assay technician loads a crucible into the gas furnace. – Placer Dome

Crucibles in the furnace. – Placer Dome

BIBLIOGRAPHY

Barnes, M. *Gold in the Porcupine.* Cobalt: Highway, 1974.

———. *Fortunes in the Ground.* Erin: Boston Mills, 1986.

———. *Timmins: The Porcupine Country.* Erin: Boston Mills, 1991.

———. *Kirkland Lake on the Mile of Gold.* Erin: Boston Mills, 1994.

Bertrand, J. P. *Highway of Destiny.* New York: Vantage, 1959.

Boyce, G. E. *Historic Hastings.* Belleville: Intelligencer Press, 1967.

Barr, E., Dyck, B. *Ignace: A Saga of the Shield.* Winnipeg: Prairie Publishers, 1979.

Blakemore, K. *The Book of Gold.* New York: Stein & Day, 1971.

Bray, M. and R. Danaher, eds. *Yesterday, Today & Tomorrow.* Sudbury: Association of Mining Municipalities of Ontario, 1991.

Brown, R. *Ghost Towns of Ontario,* vol 1., vol 2. Toronto: Cannon, 1983.

Brown, G., Brumell, N., eds. *The Ox and the Axe.* Madoc: Madoc Printers, 1983.

Buranelli, V. *Gold: An Illustrated History.* Maplewood, New Jersey: Hammond 1979.

Carrington, J., ed. *Risk Taking in Canadian Mining.* Toronto: Pitt, 1980.

Clark, H. G. *Handbook for Prospectors and Developers in the Kenora Area.* Kenora: Tri-Town Municipal Economic Development Commission, 1984.

Cruise, D., Griffiths, A. *Fleecing the Lambs.* Vancouver: Douglas & McIntyre, 1987.

Deane, P. *Manitouwadge: Cave of the Great Spirit.* Manitouwadge: Great Spirit Writers, 1989.

Downey, C. A. *A Trace of Gold.* Terrace Bay: Aquasabon Prospectors Association, 1985.

Epps, E., Bray, M., eds. *Vast and Magnificent Land.* Toronto: Lakehead and Laurentian Universities, 1984.

Featherling, D. *The Gold Crusades.* Toronto: Macmillan, 1985.

Green, T. *The World of Gold Today.* London: White Lion, 1974.

Hahn, E. *Love of Gold.* New York: Lippincott & Crowell, 1980.

Hanson, C. *Gems of the North.* Kirkland Lake: Toburn, 1979.

Hart, M. *Golden Giant.* Vancouver: Douglas & McIntyre, 1985.

Hanula, M., ed. *The Discoverers.* Toronto: Pitt, 1982.

Hindley, G. *Discover Gold.* London: Orbis, 1983.

Hoffman, A. *Free Gold.* New York: Associated Book Services, 1946.

Innes, H. *Settlement and the Mining Frontier.* Toronto: Macmillan, 1936.

Kiebuzinski, R. *Yesterday the River, A History of the Ear Falls District.* Ear Falls: Town of Ear Falls, 1973.

Keane, F. *The New Gold Rush: Canadian Gold Companies.* Munich: Roth, 1991.

Lambert, R. S. *Renewing Nature's Wealth*. Toronto: Dept. Lands & Forests, 1967.

Land, D. *Lake of the Woods: Yesterday & Today*. Staples, Minnesota: Nordell, 1975.

Lavoie, E. J. "And the Geraldton Way." *Geraldton Times Star*, 1987.

———. *Muskeg Tours: Historic Sites of the Little Long Lac Camp*. Geraldton: Squatchberry, 1987.

LeBourdais, I. *Metals and Men*. Toronto: McClelland & Stewart, 1957.

Lefoli, K. *Claims: Adventures in the Gold Trade*. Toronto: Key Porter, 1987.

Littlejohn, B., Drew, W. *Superior: The Haunted Shore*. Toronto: Gage, 1975.

Lonn, G. *About Men and Mines*. Toronto: Pitt, 1962.

———. *The Discoverers: A Fifty-Year History of the Prospectors and Developers Association*. Toronto: Pitt, 1982.

Mauro, J. M. *Thunder Bay: The Golden Gateway of the Great North West*. Thunder Bay: Lehto, 1981.

McMurray, V. *Rockhound & Prospector: A Guide to Mineral Locations in Hastings County*. Gilmour, Ontario: N. P., 1977.

Meade, F. *Through the Kenora Gateway*. Kenora: Bilko, 1981.

MacDougall, J. B. *Two Thousand Miles of Gold*. Toronto: McClelland & Stewart, 1946.

May, R. *The Gold Rushes*. London: Luscombe, 1977.

Morell, W. P. *The Gold Rushes*. London: A. & C. Black: 1940.

"N. A. Geology and Scenery: Rainy Lake and East to Lake Superior," Geological Guide #1. Toronto: Dept. Mines, 1968.

Nute, G. L. *Rainy River Country*. St. Paul, Minnesota: Minnesota Historical Society, 1976.

Nelles, H. V. *The Politics of Development*. Toronto: Macmillan, 1974.

Parrott, D. F. *The Red Lake Gold Rush*. Red Lake: Private, 1965.

———. *The Second Gold Rush to Red Lake*. Red Lake: Private, N. D.

Rasky, F. *Industry in the Wilderness*. Toronto: Dundurn, 1983.

Sabina, A. *Rocks & Minerals for the Collector: Sudbury to Winnipeg*. Ottawa: Energy, Mines & Resources, 1991.

Robinson, A. *Gold in Canada*. Ottawa: Kings Printer, 1933.

Shaw, M. M. *Geologists and Prospectors: Canadian Portraits*. Toronto: Clarke Irwin, 1958.

Schull, J. *Ontario Since 1967*. Toronto: McClelland & Stewart, 1978.

Stevens, J. *Paddy Wilson's Gold Fever*. N.L.: Upland Pedlar Press, 1948.

Towndsley, B. F. *The Mine Finders*. Toronto: Saturday Night Press, 1935.

Zaslow, M. *Reading the Rocks*. Toronto: Macmillan, 1975.

———. *The Opening of the Canadian North: 1870–1914*. Toronto: McClelland & Stewart, 1971.

PAPERS, NEWSPAPERS AND ARTICLES

Brown, L. C. "Ontario's Mineral Heritage." *Canadian Geographical Journal*, March, 1968.

Brown, L. C. "The Golden Years." *Canadian Geographical Journal*, April, 1967.

Brown, L. C. "The Red Lake Gold Field." Toronto: MNR, 1973.

Fram, M. "Continuity With Change." Toronto: Ministry of Culture, 1981.

"Gold, Policy Background Paper #12." Toronto: MNR, 1981.

"Gold Deposits of the Atikokan Area, Circular #24." Toronto: OGS, 1982.

"Gold Deposits of the Kenora–Fort Frances Area, Circular #16." Toronto: OGS, 1985.

"Gold Deposits of Ontario, Pt. 1." Toronto: MNR, 1971.

"Gold Deposits of Ontario, Southern Sheet." Toronto: MNR, 1976.

"Gold Occurrences of Ontario East of Lake Superior." Ottawa: Canada Dept. Mines, 1936.

"The Geology of Gold in Ontario, Paper #110." Toronto: OGS, 1969.

"Geology & Scenery, Peterborough, Bancroft & Madoc Area." Toronto: ODM, 1969.

Haxby, J. "Striking Impressions." Ottawa: Supply Services Canada, 1984.

Henderson, E. M. "The McKellar Story." Thunder Bay: Guide Publishers, N. D.

"Ontario Occurrences of Float, Placer Gold and Other Heavy Minerals." Toronto: MNDM, 1978.

Row, W. S. "The Illustrated History of Kerr Addison Gold Mine." Toronto: Private, 1984.

Thomas, P. "Gold." Toronto: MNR, 1981.

Weller, J. "Our Working Past: Conserving Industrial Relics for Recreation and Tourism." Toronto: Private, 1982.

The hallmark of the Royal Canadian Mint signifies the gold is 99.99 percent fine — the highest standard of any mint in the world. – Royal Canadian Mint

ACKNOWLEDGMENTS

Canada is bounded on the north by gold.

FRANCES SHELLEY WEES

John Denison came up with the idea for this book to fill an obvious gap in the literature on gold.

Companies especially helpful in the preparation of the work were the Royal Canadian Mint, Morissette Drilling, American Barrick, Greater Lenore, Freewest Resources, Christof's Jewellery, and Accurassay.

Ministry of Mines and Northern Development people who assisted were Peter Le Baron, John Scott, Don Janes, John Mason, C.E. Blackburn, Larry Turnbull, Myra Gerow, Gerhard Mayer, David Guindon, Mark Smyk, Ed Leahy, Bjarne Westin, Jim Ireland, Mark O'Brien, Ann Wilson and also Mike Cosec of the Ontario Geological Survey.

Industry professionals and production people who gave of their expertise were Hans de Ruiter, Bill Glover, George Nemscok, Alf Burns, Bill Mracek, John Haflidson, Murray McGill, Roly Lemire, Rosalie Vexina, Robert Sim, Gerard Doiron, Beth Triggs, Gord Trimble, Shelley Riley, Brian Davidson, Shelley Grainger, Otto Zavesiezky, Richard Labine, Lexi Sherman, Sheila Hilton, Glenn and Bob Kasner, Vince Borg, and Mac West.

Prospectors who took the time to talk about their work were John Larche and Don McKinnon. Ellwood Farrell offered his comments on managing McKinnon's office. Murray Pezim abandoned the stock quotations in his Vancouver office for a precious 15 minutes to talk of his experiences with prospectors.

Lynn Larocque of the Royal Canadian Mint acted as guide through a complex organization and Alistair McIntyre provided a rare tour of the highly secure Sussex Drive gold refinery.

Christof Weidner illustrated techniques of gold extraction and the crafting of jewellery from raw gold.

Dare Fowler, Bill Grozell, Real Boucher and Brenda Henderson of Morissette Drilling offered insights into the business of probing for minerals deep beneath the Earth's surface.

George Duncan of Accurassay gave a tour of the fire assay department and environmental laboratory.

Economic Development office people who were good ambassadors for their area were Twyla Gale and Dana Lewis.

Those in personal correspondence with the author were Andre Philpot, H. T. Berry, John A. Atkinson, Bob Moffat and Al Workman.

People in public and professional libraries across Ontario who helped locate material were Mabel McCulloch, Lucie Lavigne, Lynn Banks, Joyce Allick, Bryce Ross, Pia Cale, Judy Cain and Debra Burton.

There is always the fear that some person who was generous with time and resources did not receive the thanks that was their due in these pages. I hope no one who gave assistance was forgotten.

Dusk at the Williams Mine in the Hemlo. – Teck Corp.